GRANDPA'S JOURNEY

Lessons from the Kitchen
in the Art of Living Well

A. G. D'Agnese

ISBN: 1449525199
ISBN-13: 9781449525194

Dedication

This book drew inspiration from many sources.

It is dedicated to my 'kids' and to all our children.

May they all learn to enjoy their lives.

Acknowledgements

This book could not have been started without the lessons provided to me from many people. To name just a few I would like to start with my family. My 'Nona' never cooked a meal that wasn't wonderful. Rosie, my Irish grandmother, taught me that 'anything is possible to the willing mind.' To my Mom and Dad, I'll always be grateful for your love of family. And of course I must thank my children, Louis and Erin Rose; to say that I drew inspiration from our lives together borders on the obvious, but I think must be stated.

To Father William F. Burke, the mover and shaker behind the Saint Camillus band I owe a great deal.

Teachers who influenced me abound but I need to mention at least: Al Peredo my coach at Baruch College, Ed Bartley, 'Doc' Quinn, Charlie Winans, Wally Doolan and Fr. Gerard F. Giblin, S. J. at Brooklyn Prep.

To all the authors from whose books I gleaned 'Pearls of Wisdom' I hope I've done you justice and I thank you.

To Tony and Rose, I wish I could have said to you then what I know now.

Thanks to my aunt, Rosemary Murray, whose feedback and support helped make this book a reality.

For technical assistance I owe gratitude to Alex Nielsen of Northwest Outdoors in Roseburg for his fly fishing know how. And I am very pleased to be able to thank Martin Parlo, New York State Food Inspector, for reviewing the details of Brian's restaurant experience; thanks to him the 'big three' are included.

For my editors, Tricia Jones and Joe Federico, your contributions helped sculpt my simple story into a book.

To Janie Brock, your encouragement, intelligence and love kept me going. Every author should have a 'Word Nazi' as fine as you.

For courage and determination in the face of ALS I want to acknowledge my sister Rosaleen and her family. Their struggles helped, in part, to shape the ending of Grandpa's Journey.

And finally, to the crew at the Bagel Tree Café, without your inspiring dedication to delighting our customers I never would have had the time to write.

Chapters

Chapter One

The activity on the train station platform steadily increased, suggesting the northbound commuter train was due to arrive soon. People lined the platform. Like spectators at a parade waiting for the next marching band, they craned their necks and looked for a sign of the oncoming train. An older man, his dark brown hair turning gray and in some places white, wearing glasses, a light blue cotton T-shirt, faded jeans, and well-worn boots, glanced at his watch and, apparently reassured, went back to waiting. He looked around at the train station and thought how, in this country, before automobile and air travel, this same scene had played itself out so many times before.

Nearby, a middle-aged woman held tightly onto the hand of a small, freckled boy with a shock of red, curly hair. He held a bouquet of silver Mylar balloons in his other hand as he impatiently shuffled his feet and stared intently in the direction from which the train would be arriving as if willing the train to finally get there. The older man smiled and thought, 'I know just how you feel, boy. I can hardly wait myself.' From the big double wooden doors in the center of the station a large group of people joined the already waiting collection of passengers, well-wishers and greeters. They moved toward the far end of the platform and clustered together excitedly.

Frank Kilgore detached himself from the watchers and paced nervously away from the small boy with his balloons, thinking of the last time he'd spent any time with his grandson, Brian. 'Let's see. It was what? Three years ago, this December.' He had made the trip to visit his son's family in California for the holidays and had a wonderful time right up to the point when he had opened his big mouth again and upset Robert, his son, with the same old argument. He had promised himself it was not going to happen again, but between father and son there always seemed to be the same issue lurking in the shadows, just waiting to erupt and ruin the moment. He realized now that what started out as genuine concern and love had grown into an unwanted form of interference on his part. 'Perhaps, throughout Robert's childhood, I was too demanding.' In any case, he was resolved not to be judgmental in any way when Robert and the rest of the family joined them next week for the long-planned Fourth of July camping trip. In the meantime he found himself with a rare opportunity to spend some time alone with Brian.

He took a moment to appreciate what a nice day it was. The bluest blue burst upon the eye. Several high clouds drifted through the sky. A soft breeze out of the west reminded him of the phrase "as welcome as a cool breeze on a hot day" and of a friend now gone, but not forgotten. The weather for the next two weeks promised to be as wonderful as an Oregon summer could be, and Frank felt his anticipation growing for the camping trip they had planned.

A train whistle sounded from somewhere south of the station. The people on the platform pressed forward slightly to get a better look at the first sign of the incoming train. The little boy with the balloons seemed to be dancing a jig. Frank couldn't help but smile. As the train slowly approached the platform, most eyes were locked on it. Some people ready to board started to say goodbyes, while others there to meet someone were now intently watching the doors, hoping to catch the first glimpse of that special someone. Frank was no different. Hoping to recognize and welcome Brian, he wore a customary smile that was today, with good reason, broader than usual.

Shuddering to a stop, the Amtrak opened its doors and started to disgorge the passengers. Many greeters, spotting their parties, disengaged themselves from those waiting and happily reunited with their travelers. All along the platform similar scenes were repeated and a sort of shared joy filled the air. Frank spotted a tall slender teenaged boy, with light brown hair and a long, thin face, emerge from the third car and immediately knew his grandson. The boy looked remarkably like Robert at that age. Frank felt a wave of emotion sweep over him. He looked at Brian's face and watched him search among the waiting people. Their eyes met and Frank waved excitedly. Brian smiled back, but Frank knew right away something was wrong. Brian seemed tense and a little upset. As they made their way toward each other, questions started to form in Frank's mind. When they met they shared a quick hug.

"Is something wrong, Brian?"

"Yeah, Grandpa, I got ripped off on the train. I went to the bathroom and while I was gone some asshole took my backpack. I reported it to the conductor and we found the backpack but my cell phone, my iPod and video games are all gone. It really sucks. At least I had my camera on me, or that would be gone too."

"That does suck, you're right. Is there anything else we need to do, like report it to anyone?"

"No, I took care of all that already. I even borrowed a cell phone and called my mom to let her know not to expect any phone calls from me this week. Let's just get my bags and get going."

He started toward the baggage area and Frank followed closely. Brian turned his head and continued, "Not a great start to our camping trip, huh?"

"No, not a good beginning, but I hope you don't dwell on it and let it spoil our time together. The weather is going to be incredible and I guarantee you will catch plenty of fish where we're going. Why, they even call the place Fish Lake."

"Dad told me about it. He has quite a few stories about camping there with you when he was little."

"That seems like a long, long time ago."

Brian, intent on finding his bags, stepped away from his grandfather and stood waiting as the baggage was being off-loaded. He retrieved one of his duffel bags and handed it back to Frank saying, "There's just one more and we can get started." When a second, larger bag appeared Brian grabbed it and said, "That's it Grandpa, let's get a move on."

Holding the duffel bag in one hand, Frank turned toward his grandson and gave him a one-armed embrace. "I can't tell you, Brian, how much I've been looking forward to seeing you again, spending time with you and getting to know you, now that you are 'all grown up,' as they say."

"Me too, Grandpa, me too."

As they were walking toward the double doors that would lead them out of the station, Frank noticed the little boy still clutching the balloons, being squeezed by a tall, red-haired woman who was obviously his mother. The look of delight on his face spoke of his happiness and joy and reminded Frank of his own happiness. Just then the balloons slipped from his hand and drifted up into the clear blue sky. The boy grabbed at them but missed and in an instant they were gone.

The boy yelled loudly, "Your balloons, Mommy, your balloons! They're … they're gone!" He started crying, still looking up at the balloons, which were now quite high. "Oh! Those were for you, for coming home and now they're gone!" The boy cried even louder and seemed crushed by the loss of the balloons. Frank stopped near the boy and looked up at the little cluster in the sky and said loudly, "Will you look at how high those balloons are? Why, I'll bet they're already half a mile high. They sure are up there, aren't they?" Without waiting for the youngster to answer, he asked, "Do you realize everyone in Eugene will see those balloons and know how happy you are to have your mom back? That's pretty cool, I think."

The boy, confronted with this new perception, thought about it for a minute and smiled. The tears stopped, he hugged his mom, and said, "Mommy you're home." His mother looked up at Frank and mouthed the words 'Thank you,' smiled and closed her eyes to better enjoy her son's hug.

Frank turned to Brian, smiled and said, "Let's get started on this trip, eh, Boyo."

Leaving the station Brian turned to his grandfather and said, "That sure was cool what you did back there, Gramps, you really helped that little kid calm down."

"Oh, he just needed to see things in a different light is all. Most times, how we choose to look at things has a huge impact on how we feel."

Chapter Two

"I have a small boat on a trailer behind the camper, so I had to park a couple of blocks from here, where I could find a big enough spot."

"That's fine, Grandpa," replied Brian. "My legs could use the walk."

"I want to catch up with you on so much; I don't know where to begin. How's school? You're what, a junior now, right? What's your favorite subject? Are you into any sports? Oh, hell, I'm not letting you get a word in edgewise."

"No problem Grandpa, we have nearly a whole week to talk and there are some questions I'd like to ask you as well." Brian grinned at his grandfather. He said, "That's one thing dad told me, about how much you like to tell stories, er, what a great storyteller you are."

"I'm sure he warned you that I talk too much, and sometimes, I know ... I do."

"No, Grandpa, it's not like that. He told me you're a great storyteller, and that he was sure I'd have fun."

Frank nodded and pointed up the street. "Well, this is our home for the next two weeks, my boy." Frank pointed to an older, but well cared-for camper that sat on a newer model full-sized Chevy pickup. As promised, a small aluminum rowboat rested on a trailer behind the camper. The boat, which looked to be maybe fifteen feet long, if that, was loaded to the gunwales with some sort of gear, which in turn was covered by a blue tarp. "I have pretty much everything we'll need, but we should stop for ice and groceries before we head over the mountains." Frank unlocked the rear door of the camper. "Stow your bags in here."

Brian did as he was told and was surprised to see even more gear taking up most of the available space in the camper. He asked with a smile, "Do you have enough stuff, Grandpa? Maybe we need a bigger boat."

"Smart aleck kid, huh. When we set up camp at Fish Lake, you'll be glad we have every bit of that gear."

"How long will it take us to get there, Gramps?"

"If we were heading there directly, I'd guess, what with the camper and boat, maybe nine, 10 hours. But I have a little detour and a couple of stops in mind, so I don't plan on getting there for two days or so. It's not like we're on a schedule or anything, right?"

"Right … though, I thought we were just going there and waiting for my mom and dad."

"What, and miss some of the prettiest country in the world? I think not. Besides, I figured you as an adventurous type. So, I think we'll take our own sweet time getting to the Steens, and see what the Cascades and Eastern Oregon have to offer in the meantime. Okay with you?"

"Sounds great, Grandpa. Let's go."

Frank, after securing the camper, walked around to the passenger door and unlocked it. "Hop in, Brian. Your chariot awaits."

As the camper pulled away from the curb, Frank turned to Brian and said, "We are going to drive right by The University of Oregon. Don't suppose you've given any thought to becoming a Duck someday?"

"Actually, Grandpa, I have. How much of the campus can we see from the road?"

"Brian, if you want to, we'll park nearby and have a look around. What do you say about that?"

"That would be sweet."

"Sweet?"

"Yeah, sweet, eh, cool … you know … good."

"Sweet?"

"Yeah, sweet."

"In my day we'd say it was groovy."

"Groovy? Ha! No, it's sweet … or cool."

Later, after a short walk around the campus, the two travelers stopped for a couple of slices of New York-style pizza at a small pizzeria nearby. As Frank bit into his slice he tasted it, closed his eyes and said, "Oh yeah, baby, that's the real deal. This takes me back to the pizza of my youth. I grew up back in New York, you know … the birthplace of pizza. Pizza there is nothing like the stuff you get out here in the West. The crust is thin like this, and they use real mozzarella, but not so much that it overpowers the sauce, and the sauce isn't too spicy, either. None of the ingredients overpowers the others. It's the perfect marriage of ingredients. That's what makes pizza so good."

Brian, his mouth full of pizza, could only nod in agreement.

Satisfied after their snack, Frank and his grandson returned to the road and headed south on I-5, the interstate that reaches from Mexico to Canada connecting California, Oregon and Washington. Frank explained to Brian their immediate destination was to be a small town called Roseburg, where they would buy groceries, then start east across the Cascade Mountain range into Eastern Oregon. He pulled out an older, well used road map. He flipped it open and handed it to Brian. He described the route they planned on taking. "We'll take Highway 138 called the North Umpqua Highway east. It runs for a good stretch here," Frank pointed to the road on the map, "right along the North Umpqua River." Pausing, he added, "Brian, this is one of the most beautiful rivers you will ever see, especially this time of year."

Brian replied with a big smile, "Sweet."

Frank nodded at the word and returned his grandson's smile.

To Roseburg

Heading south on I-5 the countryside quickly changed from the suburbs of Eugene to farmland and forest. The road ran into some foothills where evidence of active timber production was unmistakable. Acres of hillsides that had been cut down were now in different stages of re-growth. Frank explained to Brian how much of the local economy was dependent upon lumber. "As long as people want to build new homes," he said, "and there is a market for the wood, this area will be a ready source of building materials. They re-plant in cycles and harvest the timber when it is mature. That way the resource is renewable and sustainable."

Just before they reached Roseburg, they crossed a beautiful blue-green river. Down below a series of rapids created a tapestry of white water accenting the amazingly clear river. It was dotted with people floating in little raft armadas and inner tubes, as other people played along the bank and in the shallows. Frank pointed, saying simply, "The North Umpqua."

Suitably impressed, Brian replied, "Sweet."

In the grocery store later, after they'd gotten Brian a fishing license, Frank was considering some steaks for dinner when he heard Brian chime in, "Hey, Grandpa, put that steak back, I thought I heard you say we were going to catch some fish. How about some fresh trout for dinner?"

Frank smiled, put the steak back and said, "Okay Brian, but if we're not lucky, it'll be cold cuts."

Brian just laughed and pushed the cart toward the check-out.

Before pulling out of the grocery store parking lot, Frank took a moment to show Brian, on the map, where they were headed. "The Steens Mountain is located in the southeast corner of Oregon. We actually won't be far from the Nevada border. In fact," he added, "your mom, dad and sister will be coming through Denio, Nevada, here—" Frank pointed on the map to the route that Brian's family would be following on the last leg of their trip, "—before they join us next week. We have a choice of two different routes to follow once we get to Highway 97, right here." His finger traced the first alternative as he said, "This way would take us though Klamath Falls, east from there, into Nevada, then back into Oregon, here, and then to Frenchglen, where the road to Fish Lake is. The second choice, the one I think is better, takes us north on Highway 97 to Bend, then east on Highway 20 to Burns, then on 206 south to Frenchglen." Frank rested his finger on a little dot on the map just shy of Burns, adding, "This reservoir here, Chickahominy Reservoir, can have some monster trout in it. We'll camp there for a spell before heading into Fish Lake."

"It all sounds great Grandpa, whatever you say."

To Roseburg

Chapter Three

"There's the sign for Highway 138, Grandpa. It's also called Diamond Lake Boulevard. We turn left here."

Waiting for the light to change, Frank suddenly laughed and slapped his hand to his forehead. "Of all the idiots," he said, "I forgot to buy bread back there. Oh well, we'll have to stop somewhere."

As they made the turn onto Diamond Lake Boulevard, Brian asked, "Hey Gramps, do you like bagels? There is a bagel shop right over there, The Bagel Tree Café."

"Do I like bagels? Of course I do. Remember, I'm from New York, the birthplace of bagels."

"The way you talk, New York is the center of the universe. Let's stop, Grandpa."

With camper and boat parked safely in the back parking lot, the pair entered the Bagel Tree Café through the rear entrance. The aroma of freshly brewed coffee filled the air as the pair studied the assortment of bagels that were displayed in a well-lit glass case. Frank noticed some samples on top of the case and helped himself to one. Brian did also.

"Not bad, Brian, not bad at all. A little breadier, less dense, if you know what I mean, than a true New York bagel, but the flavor is good, excellent in fact. These might be the best bagels I've had in a long time. Good idea, stopping here."

"That cream cheese has an interesting flavor too, huh, Grandpa?"

From the other side of the display case a pleasant young woman answered with a smile, "That is our world-famous Baja Cream Cheese, our own secret mix of roasted garlic, chipotle, and smoked ancho peppers. It's not too spicy but has a nice little afterburner thing that lingers on the tongue. We also have a wide variety of other flavored cream cheeses, including," she continued in an animated voice, "sun-dried tomato, garlic herb, garden veggie, and salmon; we also offer hummus, peanut butter, butter and jelly. What would you like?"

"Wow! That was impressive, young lady. You seem to be having fun today. We need a few bagels for camping and I'd like a latté to go."

"Camping, huh? Headed up the river I'll bet. I'm jealous. Which bagels would you like?"

"We'll take two sesame, two poppy and a honey wheat bagel. Do you want anything in particular, Brian?"

"Yeah, Gramps, I want to try one of these." Brian pointed to a bagel from the top shelf with peppers and cheddar cheese."

"Our Jalapeno Cheddar; would you like some Baja cream cheese to go with that?" she asked. "We have two-ounce or eight-ounce containers."

Frank answered, "Eight-ounce."

"Is there anything else I can do for you gentlemen?"

"Yeah, I'll think I'll grab an iced tea from the case over there," Brian said, nodding toward a refrigerator near the cash register.

"Okay then, that's five premium bagels, one gourmet bagel, an eight-ounce Baja, a latté and an iced tea. On that latté, would you like 12 or 16 ounces and do you prefer skim or two-percent milk?"

"Sixteen please, and could you add a little half-and-half to some two-percent for me?"

The young lady responded in an amazingly good imitation of Curly from the Three Stooges, "WHY SOITENLY."

Frank laughed heartily and repeated, "WHY SOITENLY."

Heading east on Highway 138, recalling their stop at The Bagel Tree, Frank chuckled again. "You know, Brian, that place back there reminds me of my first real job. You know that poster about the important lessons you learned in kindergarten?"

"Yeah, kind of."

"Well it's amazing to me now, but there are lessons we learn from our work too, and my first job taught me an awful lot ... things that I've carried with me all these years, lessons that have continually helped me throughout my life."

"Like what, Grandpa?"

Frank settled into a comfortable driving position, adjusted his glasses and started to reminisce. "Well, my first few jobs were not what I would consider real jobs. After doing the occasional yard work for neighbors, like every other kid, I decided that I needed to find a regular source of income. I was 14 years old and just itching to be a man. So I got a job caddying—you know, carrying someone's golf bag around a golf course for them. There was no set time to show up for work and you got paid for whatever work you did. That kind of work is just piece work. Still, I learned some things there, mainly about the value of hard work and the value of a dollar. I caddied on and off for two summers and then came my first real job at the Appetitto Shop."

"The Appetitto Shop?" asked Brian. "Tell me about it, Grandpa."

"Brian, you do realize you're asking me to tell a story, right? Once I get started—well you know I do like to talk."

"Sure, go for it."

"Okay, let's see ... where to begin? The Appetitto Shop; it's kind of funny, but no matter how hard I try, I can't remember the first time I went into the Appetitto Shop. I must have been really little. Of course, I do remember the original location, next to the old A&P on Rockaway Beach Boulevard between 90th and 89th streets. Later, it moved to between 90th and 91st streets. You might think that something that had such a big impact on my life would have made more of a first impression, but it just seems like it was always there. If you know what I mean."

Brian nodded and said nothing.

"A short, friendly Italian lady named Rose started a delicatessen that specialized in cold cuts, hero sandwiches, genuine Italian delicacies, sausages, cheeses, pasta and wonderfully fresh Italian bread. It was such good bread too. It had a hard crust, tough and full of flavor; the soft insides exploded in moist, delicious contrast. They made the best sandwiches. Rose also carried a good variety of convenience items like milk, eggs, paper goods, you know, stuff like that."

"Like the local stores you see all over now?"

"Sort of, but the cold cuts were always sliced to order, fresh, no pre-sliced, packaged stuff there. As their reputation grew so did the business. Soon, Rose's husband, Tony, quit his job and worked side by side with his little Rose. It became a true Mom and Pop success story."

"After they moved to the larger location their business continued to grow to the point that they needed more help. Their son, Simone, better known as Sonny, helped when he could … especially on Saturdays. They also hired some part-time help from among the boys of the neighborhood. Starting out as stock boys and general help around the store, some of these young men soon became skilled counter help."

Frank reflected for a moment and Brian watched as they drove past the brown, rolling hills east of Roseburg. Cattle, sheep, horses and even an occasional llama grazed in the fields as they continued on their way.

"I remember as a youngster accompanying my mother or grandmother on a shopping trip and stopping at the Appetitto. We could always count on a friendly greeting from Rose. She would give me a slice of bologna and sometimes a pinch on the cheek.

Rose treated all their customers like they were guests, which is why, I think, their business grew so quickly. As the years passed, many locals and some of the summer tourists became regulars; I know we were. When I was old enough to go to the store by myself it was to the Appetitto Shop that my mother sent me. In all my years growing up I never once dreamed how important the Appetitto would become to me."

In the passenger seat Brian sat listening to Frank as he spun his tale, admiring his grandfather's storytelling ability. He made you feel like you were part of the story somehow. Brian glanced down at the map on the seat next to him and followed their route. Noticing a point of interest, he waited for a pause and broke in, "Hey Gramps, can I ask you a question?"

"You just did."

"Ha, very funny; I really do want to hear all this, but we're coming up on a spot on the map that says Colliding Rivers. What's that?"

"Oh, yeah, there's a place up here where the North Umpqua meets the Little River kind of head-on. Do you want to stop?"

"Why not; we're not on a schedule, right?"

Just then, Brian noticed a brown road sign that read 'Colliding Rivers Boat Ramp.'

He said, "Is that it?"

"No," Frank replied, "I don't think so."

Soon, another sign announced the actual viewpoint, so Frank made a left to find a spot to park the camper.

Parking the rig in the narrow parking lot would have been difficult, so Frank drove up the road a short distance, found a place to turn around and eventually parked on the side of the road across from the Visitors Center and right above the viewpoint. Brian and his grandfather walked down to a rock wall overlooking Colliding Rivers. There indeed, the two rivers merged in a frenzy of whitewater. "Wow Gramps, look at that. There's something you don't see every day."

"No, I guess not," said Frank.

It didn't take long to see all there was to see, but the travelers agreed that just stopping like that, on the spur of the moment, was kind of neat. On the walk back to the truck Frank pointed to the Visitors Center across the road and said, "How about checking out the Visitors Center, Brian? We might get some maps or some other interesting info."

"All right Gramps, whatever."

The small wooden building had a covered porch with fir-tree shaped cut-outs that gave it a rustic, camp-like look. Inside, the pair found booklets on the waterfalls in the area, on whitewater rafting and another that described the foliage and wildlife. They also discovered two maps. One of the maps was a newer version of the Oregon road map that Frank was using and the other was a more detailed map of the North Umpqua Highway and the Cascade Mountains, including Crater Lake. Brian also picked up a brochure on Diamond Lake that proclaimed it to be 'The Gem of The Cascades.'

Frank pointed to the camper, saying, "Well, we got plenty of info, what say we get a move on?"

"Fine with me, Gramps."

After climbing back into the cab of the truck, Brian took an active interest in the booklet that described the waterfalls. He pointed to a spot and said, "There's some nice waterfalls farther up here, Gramps. This one, Watson Falls, looks beautiful." Brian held up the picture for Frank to see and asked, "What do you think about stopping to see them too?"

"I'd say you're really getting in to the spirit of adventure that will make this trip memorable for both of us and I'll be happy to stop anywhere you wish."

"Sweet."

Chapter Four

Brian read more about waterfalls while Frank pulled onto Highway 138 to continue their journey eastward. As they entered the small town of Glide, Frank spotted a gas station and decided to stop. "We might as well take the opportunity to top off the gas tank while we can, Boyo; it never hurts to be prepared."

Brian nodded without looking up from his booklet. While the gas station attendant pumped the gas, Brian pointed out to his grandfather that many of the waterfalls in the area were created when Mount Mazama erupted thousands of years ago. The eruption deposited volcanic material throughout the region and formed what is now known as Crater Lake.

"It says here that Crater Lake is the deepest lake in America and the ninth deepest lake in the world." He continued, "This picture … it's just beautiful."

Frank looked at the booklet that Brian held in his hand, then at his grandson. He smiled in response.

They soon drove out of Glide. Brian looked up from the booklet, "There sure wasn't much to that town … was there Gramps?"

"Nope, blink and you'd miss it. Just like a lot of the small towns in Oregon, small towns all over the country for that matter."

Just as Frank finished his thoughts, they approached a green metal bridge that spanned what the sign proclaimed to be the North Umpqua River. Brian looked to his right and gasped loudly, "WOW! Look at that, Gramps!"

The pair was treated to an unobstructed view of the beautiful blue-green river as it made a wide sweeping turn before passing under the bridge. The afternoon sun sparkled on clear water as the river made its way to the Pacific Ocean. The river swirled and danced around a small series of rocks near the upper portion of the turn. The lower portion held a deep pool where the water took on a much darker, placid quality. Bright shades of green from the trees lining the opposite bank, as well as the brown patches of dry grass, reflected perfectly in the deep pool. It was a picture of exquisite grandeur.

Brian couldn't take his eyes off the river as they crossed the bridge. He said, "That is amazing."

Frank replied with a huge grin, "You ain't seen nothin' yet, Boyo, the best is yet to come. That was just a preview."

"You've got to be kidding me."

"You'll see, Brian, you'll see."

The road along the next stretch teased the travelers with occasional glimpses of sunlight bouncing off the moving river. A screen of trees frequently blocked their view of the North Umpqua. Brian kept looking to his right, trying to catch a glimpse of the river as the road snaked along. Either trees or houses always seemed to interfere with a clear view.

Then, as they turned a corner in the road, they were treated to another breathtaking view of the river as it made a series of S-turns through some high rocks and gravel bars. "The color of the water is amazing, huh, Gramps? It's so clear and that green ... is unbelievable!"

Frank laughed as he replied, "Brian, this is one of the most beautiful rivers in the country, hell, in the world. Your grandmother and I spent a little time here right after we were married and we took the kids, er, your dad and aunt, once when they were about 10 or so. There are plenty of places to stop, get out and admire the view or take a picture. Anywhere you want to stop ... just let me know and I'll be more than happy to."

"Thanks, Grandpa, this is too much."

"Look at those trees sitting on top of the rocks there." Frank pointed to a number of aged white tree trunks that rested upon the rocks at crazy angles. "That should give you an idea of how high and powerful this river can get. I'll bet they got left there after the spring runoff when the snowmelt and spring rains combine to create incredibly high water."

"Yeah, and look at the old branches and stuff hung up in those trees along the bank; that's gotta be 15 or 20 feet high. There must be a whole lot of water coming through here to put that up there."

Frank answered, "It sure looks nice and peaceful now though, doesn't it?"

"It sure does."

At the top of the curve a brown sign notified travelers that the section of the North Umpqua they were now entering was restricted. Frank explained that the upper portion of the North Umpqua was for fly fishing only. No live or artificial baits could be used for angling. As if in answer to an unasked question, Brian saw a fisherman casting a fly into a likely looking pool.

"Fly fishing; that looks real interesting. I'd like to try that some day, Gramps. But I'll bet it's not as easy as it looks."

"It's not, but if you want to try your hand at it you can. I do have some fly fishing gear along. I'll teach you what I know, which isn't much, but we'll give it a shot if you like."

"Really, that'd be sweet. Thanks, Gramps."

"My pleasure, Brian, my pleasure."

For the most part the road followed closely the course of the river as it flowed west toward the ocean but for some sections the highway led the travelers through tunnels of towering evergreen trees that shut out all but a few of the sun's rays. In the deepest parts of the forest the murky floor held dark green ferns and small trees. Along the road, sunlight filtered down into the lower trees like so many random spotlights, while the upper branches were illuminated with a soft greenish glow. From the shadowy forest the camper would emerge, turn a bend and they would again be faced with a spectacular view of the river. No two views were alike and all were breathtaking.

Turning a particularly sharp curve, the road hugged the river while both ran between two high cliffs of rock. These sheer rock cliffs were mottled with green moss, ferns and some brilliant yellow-green stains. The river flowed swiftly through a series of small rapids that emptied into a deeper pool of clear greenish-blue water directly beneath the sheer cliffs. This rock face looked as if it had been folded at an angle. Right out of the cliff grew a number of trees. The largest of these trees had to be at least 100 feet tall. It was an evergreen. Another tree with pale brown bark and round, green leaves grew horizontally out of the rock. Brian had never seen anything like this before and immediately asked, "Gramps, can we stop here please?"

Frank equally astounded by the beauty of the place replied, "WHY SOITENLY!"

Just beyond the deep pool Frank observed a place to pull over and soon the two were standing on the side of the road appreciating the spectacular view. On the opposite bank, just upstream from the sheer cliff that first caught their attention, a small steam gurgled through large rocks in a flurry of whitewater to add its contribution to the main river. In silence, they stood for some moments awestruck by the magnificence of what they were seeing. Brian slowly got his camera out of its case and took a series of pictures. As he walked west on the road to get different angles he felt himself lost in the moment and in the place. He returned to his grandfather, who stood just gazing across the river. Brian noticed Frank had tears in his eyes; he cleared his throat and spoke quietly, "This is wonderful Gramps, thank you."

"Brian, I want to thank you for giving me the chance to share this with you. I'll never forget this ... special moment."

Brian, feeling himself getting a little choked up as well, said simply, "Yeah, me too."

The drive curved along the river, sometimes winding up and away into the woods, sometimes nearly skirting the water but always providing wonderful views of nature in all her glory. At one place they passed a hillside on the other bank that had obviously suffered a massive forest fire. Burned trees and charred trunks gave mute testimony to the destructive forces of nature as well as to its beauty. Soon they passed the Steamboat Inn which sat right on the river. Frank remembered that he and Moira had stayed there for a weekend to celebrate an early anniversary. They had a great time and really enjoyed all of the meals and the Inn itself. It was indeed in a beautiful location.

Later, they crossed a bridge that spanned the river. Until this point the river had been on their right; now it was on their left. There were more trees between the road and the North Umpqua and so their opportunities to view the river were less and less frequent. The road wound through tall, soaring rocks and high, white cliffs.

Frank nodded in the direction of one of these cliffs and broke the silence to say, "These white cliffs are actually compacted volcanic ash from that eruption you mentioned back there Brian, Mount Mazama. When it blew its top it deposited massive amounts of material all over this area."

"That's volcanic ash?"

"Yep, all these white rock faces are mountains of volcanic ash and pumice, sitting there for thousands of years."

Brian said nothing but referred again to the brochure he was reading earlier. After a short time he looked up to make note of the milepost. "Hey Gramps," he said, "Watson Falls is coming up soon ... keep an eye open for milepost 60; the parking area is right after that."

Chapter Five

Even on a hot summer day the nearby stream from Watson Falls and the surrounding forest provided shade and refreshment to visitors. The cool mountain air began to replace the heat of midday. Frank eased the camper and boat into Watson Fall's ample parking area and chose a spot designated for recreational vehicles. The day use area had toilet facilities and picnic tables. A sign detailed the path and viewing area for the falls and provided information about the Native Americans that lived in the area before the settlers arrived. There were a number of cars parked nearby and a large group of people were busy enjoying two of the picnic tables, which they had pulled together to form one big table. On the downhill side of the parking area, where this large group enjoyed its picnic, the forest floor boasted a wide variety of trees, shrubs and ferns. Watson Creek gurgled happily nearby. Before the truck had come to a complete halt Brian unbuckled his seatbelt, opened his door and started to get out, saying, "Just in time, Gramps; I have to pee so bad it's not funny."

Frank laughed and told Brian to go ahead. He then walked over to study the sign. He could see that to a degree, the falls could be seen from the parking lot, but to get the best view a short hike up the trail was required. As he was standing there looking up at the falls he noticed a white mini-van parking nearby. A teenaged girl got out of the passenger seat and opened the back door of the vehicle. Before she could do anything more than look on in amazement a small black and white dog sporting a black tail with a pure white tip launched itself out of the back seat and proceeded to run around the parking lot. The girl seemed concerned that the dog might misbehave and yelled in a loud commanding voice, "Tippy, get over here. NOW! TIPPY, NOW!" But the dog, excited and free from the inside of the vehicle, ran in a large circle around the parking area and almost directly into Frank.

Frank raised his arms and said in a calm voice to the dog, "Tippy, stay." The puppy, upon hearing its name used by this stranger, stopped short and started to growl at Frank. The hair on the back of its neck rose up and the dog seemed momentarily confused. This was all that the girl needed to catch up to the runaway and grab the dog's collar.

"Bad dog, Tippy, bad dog." She then smiled up at Frank as she attached a leash, "Thank you, sir, she really is friendly but she's only six months old and still not trained the way we want. All she ever wants to do is play and run. I was afraid she might get herself in trouble when I didn't get her leash on right away."

By this time, the girl's mother made it over to them and said to her, "Sarah, I've told you she can get out of hand if you let her." Turning to Frank she added, "I hope she didn't startle you, sir."

"No, I'm fine. I've had a few dogs in my day and remember what puppies can be like." He then slowly extended his hand, palm down, toward the dog, allowing Tippy to get his scent, and said in a friendly voice, "Hi, there girl, I won't bite you if you don't bite me. Okay?"

Tippy, reassured by her owner's presence and by Frank's tone of voice, sniffed at the proffered hand and wagged her tail.

"Good girl, Tippy," said the mother as Sarah reached down to pet the puppy.

Brian chose this moment to walk over to the small group. "Hey Gramps, what's up?"

"Well Brian, I just met this cute little puppy and her owners." Turning to the mother, he continued, "I'm Frank Kilgore and this is my grandson, Brian." He stepped forward and shook her hand.

Tippy pulled back against her leash when he did this and the girl had to pull on it to control the puppy. She put her hand on the dog's head and in a soothing voice said, "It's okay Tippy. Good girl."

The woman smiled and replied, "Hi, my name is Delores Trimble and this is my daughter, Sarah."

Sarah looked up and flashed a beautiful smile. "Hi, Mr. Kilgore. Hi, Brian."

"Just call me Frank."

Brian added, "Nice to meet you, Sarah." He reached down to pet the now wiggling puppy. "Hey there puppy, nice dog. Did I hear right, its name is Tippy?"

Sarah said, "That's right. This tail gave her her name." Sarah pointed to the pronounced white tip on the dog's tail. "She's quite a handful, let me tell you. She's got more energy than any other two puppies combined. She really is quite sweet though, especially when she's had enough exercise."

"Well," Frank added, "to get the best view of the falls there is a short hike up the hillside here." He pointed up toward Watson Falls and continued, "She would probably like a walk."

At the word 'walk' Tippy erupted into a wriggling mass of black and white. She whined loudly in an excited manner and looked up expectantly from Delores to Sarah to Frank.

"Oh, you said the 'W' word." Delores smiled. "Now we'll have to take her up there or she'll never let us hear the end of it. However, I'm just getting over a sore hip and I'm not walking up there," she said nodding in the direction of the falls. "I will enjoy this view and the cool air; you all enjoy your hike."

Frank smiled and shook his head in agreement, "This slope is made for young legs. I'll stay here and keep Delores company. You kids take the puppy and enjoy the walk. Brian, please take a couple of pictures for me, though. Okay?"

"Sure, Gramps." He smiled at Sarah and asked, "Okay with you, Sarah?"

Sarah smiled back and replied, "Fine with me. It sounds like fun."

"Sweet."

Brian retrieved his camera from the truck and took a picture of Frank, Delores, Sarah, and Tippy with forest and stream in the background. Reviewing his shot he noticed that his grandfather looked happy and everyone seemed at ease, except for Tippy, who constantly pulled and strained against her leash. The thought also crossed his mind that Sarah sure was pretty and really had a nice smile.

The two teens started across the parking lot with the dog toward the trail that led to the falls. Sarah constantly worked at getting Tippy to behave and while they were in the parking lot the puppy did manage to contain her excitement and heel properly. However, as soon as they entered the woods near the trailhead, Tippy caught a scent that drove her to new levels of enthusiasm. Sarah laughed and said, "She must smell a critter of some kind. Her favorite thing is to chase squirrels. I've even seen her try to climb a tree to get to one. There is nothing she likes better than a good game of 'chase the critter' or 'hide and seek'."

Indeed, even at the mere mention of squirrels, Tippy's ears went up and she again seemed convulsed with excitement.

Brian couldn't help but laugh at the puppy's antics. "She sure has a lot of energy," he noted.

"No question about that." Sarah held onto the leash trying to make her puppy behave. "Someday she is going to be a great dog. You can see she has a wonderful disposition; if she would only get over this puppy thing and learn to mind, she'd be great."

"She's just being a puppy," Brian stated, "give her some time and you'll have her trained. You seem to be doing okay with her already."

"Yeah, to a degree, but there are moments, like back there in the parking lot, when she just loses it. We'll yell at her and ... it's like ... she's got something else in her head; there's just nobody home. She'll take off on some scent or to chase a critter and be in her own little world until we catch her attention. Then she'll come running back like, okay, I'm back, did you call me?"

"She's just a puppy being a puppy. She'll learn."

Brian, walking a little ahead of Sarah and Tippy, came to a steep section of the trail and held out his hand to help steady Sarah. She reached out to accept his help and rewarded Brian with a radiant smile. Brian was aware of the warmth of her hand remaining in his long after she let go and continued on.

At the end of the trail they were treated to a beautiful view of Watson Falls. The tall, cascading waterfall sent its water tumbling down a cliff 300 feet into a jumble of rocks and pools below. From there the stream continued downhill, feeding into the North Umpqua and ultimately into the Pacific Ocean. Ferns, shrubs and small trees lined the banks of the stream. Everywhere, mature evergreens reached skyward. Moss clung to rock and tree, adding even more green to the already brilliant tapestry. Sunlight filtered through the trees and speckled the foliage, the rocks, and the water.

Brian took a few pictures and couldn't resist posing Sarah and Tippy in the foreground of Watson Falls. "Make sure you give me your e-mail address and I'll send you some of these pictures, Sarah."

"That would be really nice, Brian," Sarah said. "Thanks."

On the way back down the hill the two spoke of school, laughed at more of Tippy's antics, and shared some chit-chat until they were almost to the parking area. "Sarah, what are you and your mom planning to do next?" asked Brian.

"Well, we're going to Crater Lake. On a nice day like today the blue of the water will be absolutely incredible. And, if you've never seen Crater Lake at sunset you've never seen Crater Lake."

"I've never seen Crater Lake. This is my first visit to Oregon."

Sarah stopped and looked directly at Brian, "What were you and your grandfather going to do next?"

"We planned on stopping at Whitehorse Falls and then heading east."

"Do you think your grandfather might want to see Crater Lake? It will be breathtaking, I promise."

"I don't know. He might. Let's ask him."

Tippy made a lunge on her leash as the teens approached the parking lot, again testing Sarah's patience. "Tippy, no! Heel ... now! You stupid dog."

Brian looked up and saw the dog staring intently and laughed again. "She sees a squirrel under that picnic table."

At the mention of the word "squirrel" Tippy reared up on her hind legs and barked loudly, sending the squirrel scurrying up the nearest tree. Brian watched it move quickly from branch to branch until it jumped to another tree. It found a spot where it was no longer visible and remained in hiding. Tippy, in the meantime, threw herself into a frenzy trying to drag Sarah to the first tree. Sarah tried to make her heel. Tippy sniffed around the base of the tree and began barking nonstop.

Frank and Delores strolled over to join them, amused by the puppy's performance. "There's a classic example of barking up the wrong tree," said Frank. "This dog sure does have a lot of energy ... course now she is using it in the wrong direction."

"That's our Tippy," added Delores.

"Hey Gramps, Sarah and her Mom are going up to Crater Lake next. Do you think we should visit the only National Park near here?" asked Brian with a mischievous smile.

"Delores and I were just talking about that very thing. Do I take it you would be up for that?"

"You bet. That'd be sweet!"

Sarah laughed and repeated Brian's exclamation, "Yeah, sweet."

"Okay then, let's look at the map and see what we've got here," said Frank.

After looking over the map and the brochure on Crater Lake that Brian had picked up, Frank realized they had a problem. "There's a little difficulty with the distance involved in visiting Crater Lake, guys. We are driving a pickup with a camper and towing a boat. That's not exactly the easiest rig to tour in."

"Why don't you gentlemen park your rig somewhere and ride with us," offered Delores, "besides, that way we could use our pass and save you the entrance fee. They charge per vehicle, not per person."

"That would work," responded Frank. "Let's see … where should we park?"

Sarah suggested they leave the truck and trailer at the entrance to Crater Lake, noting that it would be visible to the park rangers that manned the entrance.

Frank looked up and smiled at her. "That is an excellent suggestion young lady; I like the way you think."

Sarah blushed at the praise and smiled back.

"Grandpa, do you think we'll still have time to visit Whitehorse Falls?"

"I think so. Besides, we do have to eat and we can make some sandwiches there while we sightsee."

"We were going to buy dinner at the cafeteria at Crater Lake," Sarah said.

"No cafeteria food for you, young lady. If you are going to drive us around, the least we can do is feed you dinner. And I won't be taking no for an answer," Frank said as he saw Delores start to object. "We've got plenty of cold cuts and some fresh bagels and it would be our privilege ..." Frank now slipped into a heavy Southern drawl, "no, ma'am, it would be our honor to share our humble repast with you wonderful ladies. Please accept our meager offerin'." Frank finished his little speech with a deep bow and a flourish of his hand, and held the position until Delores responded.

"We would be more than happy to have dinner with you gallant gentlemen. Thank you."

Chapter Six

The short drive from Watson Falls barely provided Brian with a chance to tell his grandfather about the hike up to the falls. He described the trail for Frank and laughed again at the entertaining antics of Sarah's puppy. As the truck slowed down at the entrance for Whitehorse Falls, Brian added, "And Sarah is sure cute, too."

The viewing area was just steps from the parking lot and overlooked a beautiful cascading waterfall that emptied into a pool at its base. Over time, the waterfall had carved out an area that looked like a small amphitheater. The brochure called it a punchbowl-type falls. On the opposite side of the pool was what looked like a grotto or shallow cave etched out of the rock. Many kinds of moss and ferns flourished everywhere. Wild rhododendrons and the largest trees Brian had seen thus far surrounded the area. Delores parked her car in the first parking space available, while Frank had to pull the camper and boat into a long spot along the side of the roadway.

Brian, closing the truck door behind him, noticed that Sarah was placing the leash on Tippy before letting the puppy out of the vehicle. Again, the dog seemed totally excited to be out and immediately began to look all around and sniff the air with anticipation. Brian, following the puppy's gaze, was struck by how tall these trees were.

"Gramps," he said to Frank, "I know these are not redwoods, 'cause I've been to see the tallest trees, but these sure are big. Do you know what kind of trees they are?"

"I believe these are Douglas firs, Brian and yes, they are magnificent."

"I'll say." Brian turned in a complete circle. His head lifted in wonder at the size of the trees and the way the sunlight, even this late in the afternoon, cut through the treetops and illuminated the upper branches of the trees. In some places, shafts of sunlight pierced the lower branches, brightening what would otherwise be darkened forest with an almost supernatural light, revealing tiny specks of dust, a jubilee of pixies dancing in celebration. "It's … it's like … being in church … kind of."

Frank looked up as well and after a moment, smiled and nodded in agreement.

Sarah, who by this time had taken Tippy to the area overlooking the falls and stood there with her mother, called over, "Hey, this is gorgeous; you've got to come here and see this."

Brian walked over quickly and had to agree. The pool formed by the waterfall was fairly round, with a high bank on the east side where they now stood. The water on the farther deeper section rippled with tiny waves from the waterfall, reflecting in a distorted manner the surrounding rock, tree trunks and brush. The muted pattern of browns and greens shimmering up from the pool was like a painting Brian had seen once in an art gallery. "Wow, Sarah this is like …. wow."

At the left, across the lower end of the pool, a huge tree had fallen, providing a bridge to the opposite side. Below it, a stream funneled cascading whitewater past rocks and boulders. The top of this log was stripped of bark and slightly worn down by the passage of people walking across it. A smaller log lay diagonally across the pool in front of them. Brian noticed a trail on the left that led down to the bigger log. "Let's walk down there."

"Sure, but we should wait for your grandfather," Sarah said, pointing to Frank, who walked toward them.

"Don't wait on me …. Delores, why don't you go with the kids while I fix us some sandwiches?" Frank suggested as he reached the group. "I'll be along shortly. It won't take me but a minute to fix dinner; after all, I'm a deli man from way back when."

"Are you sure you wouldn't like some help, Frank?"

"Positive. Besides there's not a hell of a lot of room in the camper right now, what with all the gear I've got in there. You go ahead and enjoy. I'll be along shortly." Without waiting for an answer, Frank walked back toward the camper.

"All right then kids, let's go; but Sarah, I would like some help on that steep part. Okay?"

"Sure Mom, no problem. Brian, would you take Tippy for me? I'll walk with my mom."

"Okay Sarah. Will she let me?"

"Tippy doesn't care much who walks her as long as she gets to go."

The little group started out on the trail. Tippy dragged Brian passed a couple of picnic tables, followed by Sarah and her mother.

"Tippy ... heel!" exclaimed Sarah upon seeing the difficulty Brian was having controlling the young dog. "Brian, tell her to heel. Sometimes she'll listen."

"Tippy, heel."

The puppy looked up momentarily at Brian and seemed to obey, but just as quickly shifted her attention when a large, black bird took flight farther up the trail. She seemed to mimic the bird by bounding into the air. Brought up short by the leash, Tippy looked back at Brian then strained against the lead.

Brian laughed and remarked, "Tippy, you have the attention span of a butterfly."

"That's our Tippy," Sarah laughed.

"That was a raven," said Brian. "It was too big to be a crow."

Before they reached the steepest part of the trail, Delores noticed a log bench that offered a wonderful view of the waterfall and the pool. "Sarah, I'll sit here and enjoy this view. You and Brian go on ahead."

"Okay Mom. We'll be right back."

"Take your time. It will take Frank at least 10 or 15 minutes to make all our sandwiches."

The trail curved down to the bank of the pool and then toward the big log. Brian noticed the water was crystal clear. The air felt cool and refreshing. Tippy went down to the water and took a long drink before seeing another raven perched on a branch in a nearby tree. Barking loudly, the young dog again made a mad dash in the direction of the bird only to reach the end of her leash with an abrupt stop. The raven slowly took off. With a few lazy beats of its wings it flew deeper into the woods, loudly squawking its displeasure.

Sarah laughed at Tippy's futile attempt to follow and said, "Nevermore, quoth the raven."

Brian laughed.

A trail of sorts led them along the bank of the stream that twisted and turned downhill. Boulders and logs funneled the riot of water first one way, then another, as it carved its way toward the river. In many places downed logs crossed the steam. Shortly, the stream made an abrupt turn and then emptied into a small pool with a gravel shore. Larger rocks were clearly visible on the bottom. A fallen tree rested on a gravel bar in the center of the stream, rotting and sporting an amazing array of moss, fungus and tiny ferns. The opposite bank was steep, with large rocks and trees whose roots could be seen growing out of the bank.

Tippy sniffed the air and walked to the water for another drink. Brian noticed a large rock shelf to his right that had a slightly deeper hole downstream. He guided the puppy over to this rock and stood on it. Small stones lying on the stream bottom were of many colors; there were reds, yellows and greenish rocks as well as the common gray and brown ones. After a moment, Brian became aware of some small fish swimming in the pool. He called over to Sarah, "Hey, there's fish in this water."

"Really?" Sarah responded as she joined Brian on the rock. "Where?"

"Right there," Brian answered, pointing to where some tiny fingerlings swam.

"I wonder what kind of fish they are," Sarah mused. "They could be trout, or even steelhead or salmon."

"I wouldn't know ... could be."

"Look Brian, a crawdad." Sarah excitedly pointed to a small lobster-like thing perched on a rock in about two feet of water in the lee of the shelf.

"A crawdad?"

"Yeah, they're also known as crayfish."

The crawdad was no more than two inches long and sat perfectly still. Sarah continued, "If you can trap enough of them you've got a tasty meal."

Brian shook his head laughing, "By the looks of this one it would take a lot of crawdads to even make an appetizer. I'll stick with lobster."

"I hear crawdads are pretty good, especially with spices and butter."

"If you say so. Speaking of food, I'm getting hungry. Let's see what my grandfather's got for us."

Frank had just joined Delores on the bench when the teens returned. The afternoon air was getting cooler, especially here overlooking the waterfall. The whole place seemed enchanted and everyone was impressed by the beauty of their surroundings. After a moment of silence, Frank remarked, "It sure is nice being here and sharing this with all of you."

"I feel the same way," said Sarah.

"Totally," added Brian.

Frank turned to Delores and asked, "When you ladies are finished with your visit at Crater Lake where are you headed?"

"Why, we'll go back to Roseburg. We're staying there with an old friend of mine from school. Why do you ask?"

"I noticed that beyond this picnic area there is a campground and there are some empty campsites. I'm inclined to grab one of those spots, leave the camper here and have you drop us off on your way back to town, if that's all right with you?"

"Sounds fine Frank; it's not out of our way at all."

"Great. At least now we know where we'll be sleeping tonight. Who's hungry? How about dinner? It's all ready and waiting right over there on that picnic table," Frank indicated one of the tables that offered a great view of the waterfall. "What say we get started?"

"Last one there is a rotten egg," Delores said as she got up from the bench.

"You can call me anything you'd like except late for dinner," Brian added as he followed the group.

Once they were all seated at the picnic table, Frank opened up the wicker basket and proceeded to pass out paper plates, napkins, plastic forks, cups and sandwiches. "Who wants turkey and who wants ham? We have some cheese as well, so if you want swiss or cheddar, it's no problem. Or … if you just want a cheese sandwich I can do that too."

"Turkey and swiss would be wonderful, Frank. Thank you."

"Gramps, can I have a ham and cheddar?"

"Absolutely."

"Mr. Kilgore, can I have turkey, no cheese?"

"Sure, Sarah, and please call me Frank."

Reaching into the basket, Frank added the cheese to the requested sandwiches and passed them out. He placed mustard and mayonnaise containers in the center of the table.

"There are some condiments if you like and we also have some coleslaw and pickles. Help yourself."

For a short time everyone focused on fixing their sandwiches the way they liked them. The nearby waterfall provided a symphony of sound as they enjoyed their food.

"Frank," said Delores, "this is delicious. Tell me, did you get these bagels in Roseburg?"

"That's right, at the Bagel Tree Café."

"I thought so. My friend made a point of taking us there yesterday when we arrived in Roseburg. She spoke very highly of it."

"I can see why. They have a good quality product and if the service we got there today is any indication, they really know how to take care of their customers. It reminds me of something I was telling Brian about earlier. My first job was in a deli back East and I learned some really important lessons there, like how important customer service is, especially when you are serving food to someone."

Sarah finished chewing a bite and paused, "Especially when serving food, why specifically then?"

"Well Sarah, when someone trusts you enough to order food from you … it's sort of a … well it's almost sacred. This is the kind of trust you might only place in family. It becomes more than just food. It is sustenance for the body and the soul because if you take their trust and do something more with it, like added service … a smile or some other gesture that shows you care … give a level of service beyond the expected … this gesture affirms their trust, and you can make their day! It's not enough to care about making customers happy … you must show them you care." Frank paused and finished, "You can take what is normally just a business transaction and transform it into something more, an event the customer will feel good about. You don't often get that kind of an opportunity with other kinds of sales. Even though I've had excellent customer service elsewhere, a person buying food is somewhat vulnerable. Great service honors the customer, and when you do your best for them it's a way to honor yourself as well."

"I've never thought about it like that before, but I think you're right."

Delores nodded in agreement and remarked, "Frank, it sounds like you had a wise teacher."

"I've been blessed with many wise teachers, including the little Italian lady that started the Appetitto Shop where I had my first job. She treated every customer as if they were her guest. You know, lessons reach us throughout our lives from many different sources. Life itself teaches you many important lessons if you are wise enough to learn them."

Brian listened to his grandfather and was impressed with the way that Sarah and Delores reacted as he spoke. They listened carefully, considered his words and weighed their meaning. Sarah nodded in agreement, and when she spoke it was with respect. "Frank, I know kids that have jobs in restaurants. A few of them seem really happy with their jobs but most treat their jobs as, well ... just jobs. I've never heard anyone speak of treating customers with so much respect before. Why do you suppose that is?"

"Maybe they haven't been trained to provide really good customer service. Or maybe they don't understand how important their job could be. I was lucky. I had a wonderful teacher in my first job who opened my eyes. I have benefited from those lessons all my life."

Delores smiled at Brian and spoke to him. "Your grandfather has not only provided us with a great meal in an absolutely beautiful place but has given us some real food for thought. I consider it our good fortune to have met you two."

Brian smiled back at Delores, feeling proud of his grandfather.

Chapter Seven

After dinner, Frank drove into the campground and found an empty campsite. He parked the rig after unhooking the boat, filled out the campsite permit and paid for one night's stay. After carefully looking around, he had Brian help him push the boat behind and to one side of the camper. Nodding in satisfaction, he locked his truck and announced, "Okay, we're all set. Let's go see Crater Lake."

From Whitehorse Falls the road to Crater Lake steadily gained elevation. The lush evergreen forest of pine and fir trees gradually gave way to a high alpine forest that seemed stunted in comparison. Brian made a comment about how the trees seemed different. "Do you notice that the size and type of trees are changing?" he asked.

"This high up, snow comes earlier in the fall and in the spring melts much later," Frank answered. "There doesn't seem to be as much underbrush up here either."

Brian rode in the back seat behind his grandfather. He watched the trees roll by while stealing an occasional glance at Sarah. Tippy rode in the middle, staring intently ahead. The early evening light cast shadows into the road. Rounding a long, gradual curve, Delores suddenly tapped the brake and pulled the vehicle to the left. Up ahead and near the road on the right a number of deer stood browsing.

"I am deathly afraid of hitting a deer."

"Hitting a deer is dangerous," said Frank "and certainly won't do your car any good, but you really have to be careful not to overreact. It's still better to hit a deer than run off the road. Delores, you did just fine."

Tippy jumped onto Brian's lap trying to get her head out of the window to see the deer. He laughed as he struggled with the puppy until Sarah reached over and grabbed her dog.

"Tippy, you dumb mutt! Get off of Brian. Come here now."

"She's okay. She just wanted to see the deer."

"Yeah, but she has to learn to behave; she really does."

Soon, after turning onto the road for Crater Lake and presenting their National Park pass at the ranger station, they made their way up toward the lake. Sarah had saved a guidebook from an earlier visit and referred to it now. "We're coming up to the Pumice Desert and it won't be long before you see Crater Lake, Brian. There is a viewing area for the Pumice Desert on the right, but we really don't have a lot of extra time to stop."

In a short while, Delores pulled into a viewing area with an unobstructed view of the lake. A short rock wall defined the parking area and a number of other vehicles were already parked facing the lake. Before opening the door Sarah struggled to get the leash on Tippy. "There will be no running off for you this time, little missy. You're staying with me."

Once out of the car, they were treated to an amazing view of Crater Lake. The sun lit up the farther side of the lake and the sides of the crater. The clear, dark blue water reflected the turquoise sky. The blue water on the near side of the lake was already in shadow and took on a deep, almost purple color. Along the shoreline, the water seemed blue-green. The overall effect was breathtaking. Off center in the lake, near the southern shore, a small island rose out of the deep blue, with lighter blue rimming its shores.

Brian closed the door behind him without ever taking his eyes off the beautiful view. "Wow! I've never, never seen anything like this before. This is awesome."

"I told you so," Sarah bragged as if she were responsible. "There's nothing like Crater Lake."

"I'll say."

Tippy suddenly barked in a frenzy and strained against her leash. A type of ground squirrel that looked like a chipmunk sat on the rock wall about 10 feet from where they stood. The puppy was wild with excitement. The ground squirrel scurried over the wall and was soon gone, but the puppy continued to fight the leash, desperate to chase after it. Sarah yanked on the leash until the young dog was brought up short and yelled right in her face. "Tippy! Tippy, no! SIT NOW ... TIPPY BEHAVE!"

Finally, the pup shifted her attention to Sarah and settled down. But every once in a while, as they all stood admiring the view, Tippy looked at the wall where the small animal had been.

Delores started back to the car and said, "I want to show you another viewpoint on this side before we drive over to the northeast side of the crater for sunset. Let's load up, gang."

Higher up on the west side of the crater, a larger parking area offered a different but equally spectacular view. From this viewpoint the lake, which was easily 600 or 700 feet below could almost be seen in its entirety. Again, a rock wall separated the parking area from the steep sides of the crater. Brian, fascinated by the spectacular view, opened his door without taking his eyes off the lake. As he stepped around the car door, he felt Tippy race past him, followed by Sarah's command. "Tippy, heel! Tippy. Tippy NOW!"

Brian glanced to his right only to see the puppy vault over the wall in pursuit of a small squirrel. Instead of going to ground near the wall, the squirrel ran quickly away from the parking area and the following puppy. Its path led out to a rocky point that sat high over a steep slope of loose rock and pumice. Tippy chased the squirrel happily, unaware that every step she took kicked up small stones and pumice that rolled down the slope, over the edge of the rim, and fell at least 600 feet to the waiting rocks and lake below. The loose rock shifted beneath her feet. Sometimes her paw slipped as she raced in pursuit. Brian watched as Tippy chased after the squirrel and hoped she wouldn't fall.

Delores, standing near the front of her car, held her hand over her mouth, her eyes startled wide in disbelief. Sarah meanwhile, ran to the wall and continued to yell at the puppy. "TIPPY! COME NOW! TIPPY NOW! But the young dog had a squirrel in her sights and completely disregarded her commands. As all watched in shock, the puppy followed the fleeing squirrel around the rocky point and was lost to view.

Frank stole a glance at Brian and realized that his grandson felt responsible for allowing the puppy to get out of the car before Sarah could get its leash on. Sarah was frantically calling to her dog while Delores continued to stare at the rocky point, the rim of the crater and the steep drop-off in a mixture of horror and foreboding. Frank quickly stepped over to Sarah and tapped her on her arm. "Sarah, walk with me up here where the slope is not as steep so when she returns she'll have an easier trail back to you."

Sarah continued to call out for Tippy but nodded yes toward Frank as she accompanied him to where he'd indicated. Tippy had been barking nonstop as she chased the ground squirrel. Her barks could still be heard echoing off the rim of the crater. They all listened and watched intently for some sign of the puppy's return. When the barking stopped Frank held his breath. After what seemed a long time but was really only seconds, Tippy came trotting around the point, black tail wagging, white tip fluttering, her red tongue lolling, with what Frank could swear was a happy grin. She saw Sarah and Frank near the wall and finally responded to Sarah's commands to come. As Sarah placed the leash on the dog, she yelled at Tippy for not coming when called, but Frank could tell she was more relieved than angry.

Brian walked slowly up to Sarah, hesitated before speaking and apologized for forgetting about Tippy and opening his door before

Sarah could attach the lead. "She was out before I even thought about her, Sarah. I'm really, really sorry," he said again.

"That's okay, Brian, she just doesn't mind well enough when she should. She better learn soon or I don't want to think about what could happen next time." To Tippy, Sarah spoke firmly, "Tippy you listen to me when I tell you to come. You hear me, dog?" Tippy looked up at Sarah and wagged her tail.

At the next viewpoint Sarah had the leash on Tippy before they finished parking and the group was treated to an incredible sunset. As sunlight slowly retreated up the sides of the crater, the stunning hue of Crater Lake changed from deep blue to purple. The farther sides of the crater took on a reddish bronze color until the sun was completely gone. Red-streaked clouds added their mark on the scene even after the sun had set. The moments seemed endless as they watched nature showing off.

In the car later, on the way back to Highway 138, Brian sat quietly while the rest of the group talked about how beautiful the sunset had been. "I loved how the color of the lake changes from that startling blue to purple and then to gray as the sun sets. It seems like it takes a really long time, but once the sun goes down it only takes minutes," Sarah said.

"I'm always blown away by the amazing wonder of the place," added Delores.

"I'm very impressed as well. What about you, Brian? You're awfully quiet back there. What impressed you the most?"

"Oh, I don't know, the blue of the water I suppose. That is an amazing color. I was thinking about how immense Mount Mazama must have been and how violent its eruption was to form Crater Lake. The road around the crater, what they call the Rim Drive, is 33 miles long. The lake itself is seven miles across. We passed huge hills of ash and pumice on the way here and the leaflet on the waterfalls said they were formed by that eruption as well. I'll bet that was a sight, what 7,000 years ago?"

"Not all that long ago in geologic time, actually," answered Delores. "There were probably native witnesses to that eruption."

"I wonder what they would have thought about it," Sarah remarked.

"Probably that their god was angry or something," answered Brian.

Later, Frank asked Delores to stop at a little market he had noticed on the way up so he could buy some firewood for the night. "It ain't camping without a campfire."

Frank and Brian went into the store while Delores stayed in the car with Tippy. Sarah went to use the restroom. In the store, Brian noticed some animal heads mounted on the walls. There were deer and bear heads and even a cougar was displayed there. Pointing to a big buck with an impressive sets of antlers he said, "That deer looks a lot bigger than the deer we saw by the side of the road, huh, Gramps."

"Well, yes it does."

The young man behind the counter informed them that the deer to which they were referring was a mule deer, a species that lived primarily on the east side of the Cascades, while the deer that lived on the west side were mostly the much smaller blacktail. "That particular deer was taken by my father over in the Steens."

"That's where we're going," Brian replied, "to Fish Lake."

"Sure is pretty country over there … some mighty big deer," the young man said. "Have a nice trip."

Soon, back at their campsite, it was time to say farewell to their new friends. Frank and Brian took turns petting Tippy and after some small talk finally said their goodbyes. "Delores, Sarah, it was a real pleasure meeting you and sharing this time with you. I hope you enjoy the rest of your trip and I want you to know how much I enjoyed our adventure. Drive safely."

"Frank it was our pleasure, and you two guys have fun on your trip. Brian, you're a nice young man; have a great time with your grandfather."

"Yes Ma'am, I will. And Sarah, I'll e-mail you those pictures. I sure had fun. I hope that dog of yours learns to hyper down some day."

"Thanks, Brian. Yeah, if she doesn't settle down soon she'll end up driving me crazy."

"Well, at least that would be a short trip." Brian smiled and waited for Sarah to respond. He didn't have to wait long.

Sarah laughed and playfully punched Brian in the arm saying, "You're a real funny guy, huh? Have fun camping, okay?"

"Sure."

With that Sarah, her mother and the puppy got into their car and drove out of the campground.

Chapter Eight

"Setting up camp tonight won't take long kiddo, mostly clearing out some of the gear in the camper, getting a campfire going and relaxing a while before bedtime. How's about a hand?"

"Sure, Gramps, what should I do first?"

"Climb into the camper and take out the stuff that's in the aisle so we can get to the beds. That plastic bucket right there has a lantern in it. Get that out first and we'll put some light on the subject."

"Okay." Brian handed out the bucket and while Frank got the lantern going, cleared the camper floor by placing the rest of the gear on the picnic table. "This stuff will be okay here, won't it Grandpa?"

"Yep; in fact that's a good place for it. We can cover it with a tarp and in the morning just put it back inside the camper."

In a short while, Frank had the camper ready. He went to the campground's bathroom facilities and brought back a bucket of water. "This will do for cleanup later. I have a pretty large water tank in this thing but it never hurts to conserve that water for drinking and cooking." Then he used some old newspapers and the wood he'd bought to start a small campfire. Frank pulled out two folding chairs from among the gear in the boat, and set them up near the fire.

Overhead, a cool evening wind whispered through the branches of the trees. The sound of the waterfall and the murmuring of the nearby stream provided all the music needed. With nightfall, the heat of the day was replaced by a definite chill. Frank got up, went to the camper and grabbed a fleece from inside. He called out to Brian, "Hey kiddo, do you need a sweatshirt or a light jacket?"

"Sure, Grandpa, I have a green jacket right on top in my bigger bag. Thanks."

Zipping up his fleece, Frank handed Brian the jacket and moved his chair a little closer to the fire. The fire pit began with a metal corner that held a grate. Volcanic rocks, 12 to 14 inches high, completed the circle. The fire threw off just enough warmth to cut the chill and provide some light. The flickering firelight lent a red glow to their faces as they sat silently for a time, each lost in his own thoughts.

Sometime after they sat down, a truck pulled into the campsite next to them. A family noisily began setting up its camp. Brian used this interruption to ask Frank a question. "Gramps, this has really been a great day. I saw some of the most beautiful scenery I've ever seen. But you started to tell me about the Appetitto Shop before we got to Colliding Rivers and never finished your story. Of course, you said some stuff at dinner that was from there, right?"

Frank nodded and allowed Brian to continue.

"Well, I'd like to hear the rest. Okay?"

"Sure. Now where was I ... oh, yes ... I told you about the Appetitto Shop and how it started and grew. I mentioned how I learned some really important lessons there. Let me tell you about how I got hired." Frank sat back in the chair, stretched out his legs so that his feet rested against the fire pit and looked up toward the treetops before continuing. "I was almost 17 ... by then Rose wasn't feeling well all the time and couldn't work her normal schedule. Tony ran the store with a couple of full-time employees, a rare appearance by Rose, Sonny on Saturdays, which was the busiest day of the week, and some part-time kids. One of my friends, Charlie, worked there."

"One day, when I was in the shop picking up some groceries for my mom, Tony spoke to me. He looked me straight in the eye and told me he would need a new stock boy and would I be interested. He knew my parents, he said, and thought I might be a good worker. He explained the starting pay and what hours I would be expected to work. He went on to tell me the job had potential for growth since most of the stock boys eventually became counter help, which paid more."

"Without hesitation I accepted. To be sure, I felt a little intimidated but the job didn't seem too complicated so I thought it would be okay. I remember running home to tell my mom I had a job. I'll never forget the pride I felt as I told her I was going to work at the Appetitto Shop."

"What was your mom like, Grandpa?"

"Oh, Mom was a big woman who worked hard all her life. She put herself through nursing school and when I was little, was a pediatric nurse at one of the local hospitals, working 11 at night till seven in the morning. Mom had a great sense of humor and a gap right between her front two top teeth. You never saw anyone who could spit water farther or more accurately than your great-grandmother." Frank laughed softly. "She was a real sweetheart." Frank paused for a minute and stared for awhile into the fire before adding a piece of wood.

"Well then, where was I? Oh, yes ... I'd like to be able to say I never gave Tony any reason to regret hiring me, but that simply wasn't the case. At first, the main job I had was stocking shelves. On my first day, Tony had placed some cases of canned goods in front of their respective rows and showed me how to open the case with a box cutter. He instructed me to place them correctly on the shelves after rotating the older stock toward the front; pretty simple stuff, right?"

Brian nodded yes.

"I thought so too. When I was finished I reported back to Tony and told him I was done. Instead of giving me another job to do as I expected, Tony smiled and said okay, let's see.

We went back to the shelves and Tony carefully looked at the job I had done. Well, he said, this looks almost good … almost good. I want you to notice a few things about these products. Do you see how not all the labels are facing out perfectly? And, he continued, do you see how some of these older cans have a little dust on them? See where this line of canned peas isn't exactly straight? Now, none of these things is a big deal … right? But … when I think of what the Appetitto Shop means to our guests, I want things just right. I want our customers to feel like we do everything to the best of our ability. If they see that we do the little things right, they'll have confidence that we do the important things right too. If we do everything we can, even the little things … especially the little things, the best we can … it's another way of saying that they are welcome here and we appreciate their business."

"Tony said nothing more to me. He handed me a towel, smiled and returned to the front counter. I set about dusting all the cans that needed dusting. I straightened out and faced all the other cans, even on product I hadn't restocked. When I was finished I looked around and was proud of what I had done."

"Right about then, Tony poked his head around the aisle, looked at the shelves and smiled. Good job, he said, I like what you've done. Any chance you might do it a little faster next time? I need you to deliver some groceries right now."

"As I learned the job and got better and faster at my tasks I found Tony more willing to add to my responsibilities. One day, after I had broken up some boxes, he showed me where the Coke, Pepsi and other soft drinks were stored in an old bungalow behind the store itself. Carry two cases at a time, no more, he cautioned, to the refrigerator up front and re-stock the case. Make sure they're all clean and pull some cold ones out to leave in the front so a customer doesn't get a warm soda. On about my fourth trip back to the storage room I stopped for a breather. Before long, Tony came and found me. He didn't look pleased. Son, he said to me, I don't mind you taking a short rest but I don't want to have to wonder where you are. When you want a break from now on I expect you to ask me. I'm saying this because here at the Appetitto Shop we're a team. If you're going to be a good teammate then you have to think about the other members of the crew. You've been working hard and it is hot, but Charlie is due for a break first and I was waiting for you to finish before I sent him. Understand? I said I did and quickly got back to work. When I brought out the last two cases I noticed Charlie giving me a strange look and I knew I'd hear more from him. I wasn't wrong."

"After helping close the store Charlie walked me home. You know, he said, Tony isn't sure he made such a good decision hiring you. He put up his hand to stop me from interrupting and continued; we don't have a big store so we really have to work hard and fast. It can be really hard work especially when we get really busy ... and the hotter it gets, the busier we get. By the way Brian, the Appetitto was not air-conditioned like all the stores are now. Anyway, Charlie let me know I couldn't slack off without letting everyone else down. I thought about that for a while and decided I wanted to take more pride in myself than that ... so from then on I worked harder and asked whenever I needed a break."

Brian stood up and stretched, still listening to his grandfather's story. He reached over and grabbed the last piece of wood and looked to Frank for an okay as he held it over the fire. Frank nodded yes and resumed his tale. "I learned so many valuable lessons at the Appetitto Shop and today I'm amazed at how some of those lessons, learned so long ago, have influenced me and helped shape my life. For instance, I remember one day—Rose happened to be in the store—Tony took me aside saying he wanted to show me how to make a sandwich. He taught me how to properly cut the bread, slice and stack the meat, add the cheese, the condiments and wrap it. Then, when the next customer came in and ordered a hero— that's what sandwiches on Italian bread are called back East—he watched as I made my first sandwich for a paying customer. I recall being nervous and taking a long time to get it done, but when I was finished, Tony smiled and told the customer that he was receiving my very first effort. Everybody laughed. Afterwards, Rose said something I'll never forget. She placed her hand on my forearm and said, you just provided one of our guests with food, but it's not just fuel for his body, it is also sustenance for his spirit. You see, I believe when we prepare a sandwich for a customer we're not merely satisfying the need a person has to eat. We're doing much more than that. Anyone who orders food from us … trusts us to give them clean, healthy food prepared especially for them. We prepare this food using the freshest ingredients and present it to them to enjoy. It is this trust and enjoyment that makes our job so special. There is an intimacy involved in buying food that you just don't have when you buy a shirt or something like that. It should make you happy and proud when you satisfy our guests. You know Brian, I'll never forget that talk. I was impressed with her sincerity and the respect she had for our customers. I understand now that delighting our customers was really what my job was all about."

"You mentioned this at dinner, Gramps. You also said something else about how providing good customer service honors the customer and honors yourself. I didn't quite get that part. What do you mean?"

Frank looked up at Brian, and smiled. "Well now, that's a good question because to answer that question we have to examine the definition of the word 'honor.' It's getting late now and we should get ready for bed. Tomorrow, I'd like you to look up honor. I have a dictionary in the camper, and we'll continue this talk then. Okay?"

"Okay Gramps, whatever."

"Great. I'm going to take a short walk over to the facilities and brush my teeth. You can wash up here or go on over yourself … whichever you'd like. When we're done we'll douse the fire with the leftover water and turn in."

Inside the camper Frank pointed to the large bed that rested above the cab of the truck. "That's yours for now, Brian. I'll sleep on this bed." He indicated where the table was.

"What bed Grandpa?"

"Oh," Frank chuckled, "The table comes out and the seat cushions make a bed. In fact, you can help me pull this up." Frank took hold of one side of the table and waited for Brian to lend a hand. Soon both beds were ready and Frank pulled two small flashlights out of a drawer. "Here Brian, take one of these in case you have to get up in the middle of the night."

"Thanks Gramps."

"Time for sleep, huh, Boyo, I'm bushed."

"Yeah, I'm tired too."

Turning off the lantern plunged the camper into total darkness. Brian tried to see his hand in front of his face and could not. "Wow, this is dark. I can't ever remember being in such complete darkness before, Gramps."

"Listen to the waterfall, Brian. By the time your eyes get accustomed to the dark I'll be asleep. Better yet, close them and go to sleep yourself."

Brian lay in bed and listened to the gentle sound of the water and of the murmuring of the wind in the branches. The cool fresh air softly brushed a curtain against his cheek. He snuggled down into his sleeping bag and heard one more sound that made him smile. His grandfather's gentle snoring was the last thing he remembered before drifting off himself.

Chapter Nine

Daylight was at least an hour away when Frank woke up. He lay still not wanting to disturb Brian. He relived some of the moments from the previous day and again appreciated the beauty and wonder he experienced. He thought about his grandson. He believed he saw something good in Brian. The boy carried himself with poise and dignity. He seemed to be sensitive to how others felt. His concern over the incident with the puppy at Crater Lake proved that. During conversations, Brian listened, asked questions and evidently made an effort to understand what was being said. When he spoke, he was clear and to the point. Frank tried to remember what he had been like at that age and realized that too many years and experiences lay between then and now for a valid comparison. 'Besides, times are sure different now. I need to learn more about this boy before I go spouting off.' He felt certain spending more time with Brian would be a pleasure. Today, they planned to make camp at Chickahominy Reservoir and get a little fishing in. Frank started to go over all the things that needed to be done and realized he was overdoing it.

After some time, and more than one attempt to get back to sleep, Frank realized that he might as well get up. He dressed slowly, rolled up his sleeping bag and left it on the bed. As quietly as possible, he opened the door of the camper and squeezed the door shut so it didn't make a sound. Once outside, Frank stood near the camper, pulled on his fleece and drew in several deep breaths, exhaling deliberately and completely each time. He turned and made his way toward the waterfall. He stood in the predawn gloom listening to the waterfall's symphony of sound. The white, churning water in the pool was clearly visible even in the murky early morning. Frank smiled and followed the trail until he came to the bench that overlooked the pool. Sitting down, he thought, 'This'll be a good place to wait for dawn.'

Talking about the Appetitto Shop the day before brought back so many memories. He thought of Tony and Rose; the impact they had on his life was immeasurable. He didn't realize how important they had both been to him until well after Rose had passed away and he'd lost contact with Tony. 'I'm sure Tony has joined her by now; hell, Sonny is an old man by now. Hell, I'm almost an old man myself.'

Frank had definite ideas about some things. A few of his beliefs, he knew, came from lessons he had learned on his first job from his old boss. He learned there that excellence is a process and a habit; that the world is full of wonder and life must be lived every day and in every moment. He smiled and remembered something Tony would say, "The best lessons are the ones we learn for ourselves, but we should learn from the mistakes of others 'cause we'll never live long enough to make them all ourselves."

He also learned that the way a person chooses to live should contribute in some way to the world and be with honor. Honor; there's that word again. And now Brian wants to know. 'I'm extremely grateful to have this opportunity. What will be the best way to get this across to Brian? We'll just have to see. It will depend on him; just as it always does, just as it must. This is one of those lessons that can only be learned when one is ready, willing and able.' Frank recalled a poem he had that would help if the subject came up and smiled when he remembered that he had a copy of it in the camper. Its name was 'Perpetual Caterpillars.' He thought, 'My grandson won't be one of those, not if I can help it.'

Frank sat on the bench. Captive to his memories and deep in thought, he did not notice the dawn as it materialized around him.

Brian awoke to the sound of a little girl crying. For a brief moment he thought he was in his own bed and his little sister was crying. He was about to call out to her when he remembered where he was. His mind muddled with sleep, he rolled over, pulled his sleeping bag over his head and tried to doze.

"Daddy, tell him to give it back. Billy took my doll's car," the little girl whined between sobs, "and he hit me."

"I did not. I took her stupid car but I didn't hit her," Brian heard Billy reply.

A man's voice from inside the tent nearby commanded, "Both of you be quiet. People are trying to sleep."

Brian smirked and thought, 'Yeah, people are trying to sleep.' He pulled his head out and looked over to see if his grandfather was awake, only to find him gone. His sleeping bag, rolled up, rested on the bed, but there was no sign of Frank. 'I might as well get up. That little girl isn't going to stop crying till her mom gets up.' He swung his legs over the edge of the bed and sat there a moment. Soon enough, a woman's voice called from the tent. "Come here, honey. What's the matter?"

Brian chuckled and said aloud, "I knew it. They're so predictable."

Carefully climbing down from the bed, Brian located his duffel bag and got dressed. He was just tying his shoes when the camper door opened and his grandfather stuck his head in.

"Good morning, sleepyhead. Oh, you're already up. Sleep well?"

"You bet Gramps. I slept like the proverbial log. How'd you sleep?"

"Very well, thank you. I woke up early, and sat listening to the waterfall as morning broke. It's really a wonderful spot."

"It sure is."

It didn't take them long before they finished off the remaining bagels with some cereal and juice, cleaned up after breakfast and began to load up for the next leg of their journey.

"Packing this stuff back in the camper is like a science project, Brian. Things have to be snug or they'll shift. In fact," Frank added, "these drawers are designed not to open by accident while we are bouncing around on some dirt road. See how you have to lift up and then pull to open them." He demonstrated the right way to open a drawer in the camper as he spoke. "All trailers and campers have drawers like this."

"Let me try that," responded Brian, and after a moment of fidgeting, he figured out how they worked.

"So, all that gear on the table needs to go back just the way it was. Would you start handing it to me, one at a time ... oh, and the lantern goes in last. Of course, I expect to be in camp by mid-afternoon but old habits, you know."

"We'll have time to fish then, right?"

"Yes, we will."

"Sweet."

As soon as the camper had been loaded it was time to hitch up the boat. "Grab the other side of the boat and help me pull it up to the hitch. I'll hook this thing up and we can be on our way."

"Okay, Gramps."

The truck, camper and boat trailer could not travel as quickly as most of the other traffic, particularly uphill, and Frank sometimes pulled over to let traffic pass. On the east side of the Cascades, Highway 138 provided a fairly straight route until it ended at Highway 97. Since it was mostly downhill, they made good time.

Once they turned north on Highway 97 they encountered a lot more traffic and Brian noted how many trucks used this road.

"Highway 97 is the other main north-south highway in this state, Brian," Frank explained, "and it is pretty heavily used. When we get to Bend, we'll have some lunch and once again head east … on Highway 20. Chickahominy Reservoir is maybe three-and-a-half to four hours beyond that."

Brian studied the map and said, "It looks like we've got a good hour before Bend. Gramps, why don't you tell me more about the Appetitto Shop. And how is doing a good job a way to honor yourself?"

"I'm glad you're interested. Let me begin by asking you a few questions. Okay?"

"Sure."

"Good. Can you tell me what the word 'respect' means?"

Brian spent a little time thinking about the best way to answer. He replied, "To have a high opinion of somebody is to respect them. Right?"

"Very good; that is one of the definitions of respect. But like many words in the English language this word has different meanings, depending upon how it is used in a sentence."

"You're talking about context, right? We studied that in school."

"Yes … and no. A word is just a collection of letters. Somewhere along the way we have all agreed that the word 'road' should be used to describe this thing we are driving on. What's important is that we agree. So when I say 'road,' your understanding of that word leads to an understanding of what I'm trying to say. Follow me so far?"

"I … think so."

"All right then, sometimes if I use a certain word in my sentence a listener might think I'm saying one thing, when really I'm trying to say something else. Has this ever happened to you?"

"Well yeah … sure it has. Actually, it happens all the time. You just figure out where the misunderstanding is and say it right."

"Good. So by saying something a little differently, you come to agreement."

"Yeah, I guess."

"The point is that a lot of grief could be avoided if we knew from the start how to agree on the words we use. I'm talking about real communication here. Most of the problems people have really understanding one another is that they assume they know what the other person is trying to say and that assumption, um, flavors … their interpretation of the message. Look, I don't want to spend a lot of time on this, I just want to make the point that in order for us to really communicate, I'd like to be sure we agree on the words we're using; to do that I'm going to need your involvement. I would like you to share this process with me. Okay?"

"All right, I'm game."

"Great. I have a dictionary along." Frank tapped a book on the seat of the truck. "Look up the word 'respect'."

Brian picked up the old dictionary and thumbed through it until he came to 'respect.' He thought his grandfather was getting a little weird about this whole word thing, but he was willing to go along with it for a while. "Here it is Gramps; respect … wow! For a little word it sure has a lot of meanings." Brian spent a few minutes reading all the definitions of the word 'respect' as well as its synonyms and antonyms. "Respect as a noun means admiration, esteem, reverence, and to have a high opinion; as a verb it means to value something, to show consideration for, appreciate, obey, acknowledge and accept. That's kind of interesting, Grandpa."

"I'm glad you think so, Brian. The reason I started with respect is because I want you to know that I respect you. You as a person … as a teenaged boy … as my grandson; I respect your right to your own opinions and I respect your right to disagree with me."

"Thanks Grandpa. I respect you too."

"Good." Frank smiled as he drove and waited a short time before continuing, "Okay, I'll bet you're wondering how this relates to the Appetitto Shop? I'll tell you. I had a similar conversation with Tony about a week after Rose had given me her little talk about how satisfying a customer should make me proud. He stopped me just as we were leaving at the end of a busy day. I was hot, tired and wanted nothing more than to go home, throw on a bathing suit and go for a dip in the ocean. Tony said he watched me work and that he thought I was doing better. But, he asked me, was I proud of myself? I quickly said I was. Tony said, son, I know you want to get going. So do I, but I don't think you know the answer to that question because I really don't think you've given it enough thought to come up with a good answer. Here's what I want you do. Sometime in the next couple of days I want you to look up the word 'pride' in the dictionary. Study it. Understand exactly what the word means and all the ways it can be used. Next Saturday I'll ask you again. Then, you can give me a real answer."

"Well, I didn't get right around to it but a few nights later I was doing some homework. I had to use the dictionary for another word and I found myself looking up 'pride.' What I found was interesting. I thought I knew what 'pride' meant. But when I studied it as Tony suggested, I found a new way of understanding the word."

Frank drove for a time without adding anything. Brian sat watching the scenery speed by. It took him a while before it dawned on him to look up 'pride' in the dictionary. Sheepishly he opened up the book and found the word. Frank glanced over at the boy and grinned.

Brian read for some time. Frank watched as he began to look up other, related words. Occasionally, Brian would mutter out loud and go back to a definition, then thumb the pages quickly to another. Frank nodded his head in appreciation as the boy explored the word. After a while, Brian closed the book, put it down and looked

To Bend

out the window. The high desert of Eastern Oregon whizzed by as they made their way north.

"Hey Gramps, what kind of music do you have along?"

"Music … why, there's classical, Vivaldi, Mozart, Bach and Beethoven … What's the matter? Don't you like classical?" Frank asked as Brian rolled his eyes.

"What else, Gramps? Classical is okay but I'm not in that kind of mood right now."

"Okay then, how about a different kind of classical? Led Zeppelin's greatest hits; Classic rock and roll."

"Now you're talking … play that."

"As you wish."

Chapter Ten

"-And she's buy…uying a stai…airway to…hea…eaven." Brian sang along with one of the songs he recognized from the CD. Frank drove on, smiling and tapping his fingers to the music.

"Hey, Gramps did you see that sign? We're coming up on the Oregon High Desert Museum. How about stopping?"

"We can Brian, but if we do, it'll cut into our fishing time this afternoon."

"Oh … never mind then; I want to fish."

Frank chuckled, "Glad to see you have your priorities in order, Boyo."

"I am getting a little hungry, though. How soon is lunch?"

"Bend is still a ways. I suppose we could stop for gas and you could grab a snack. I'll find a gas station with a mini-mart."

"Sweet."

Slowly pulling up to the pump, Frank said to Brian, "Here's five bucks; while I get gas and hit the bathroom, go get yourself something and buy a couple of bottled waters. Okay?"

"Okay, Gramps."

Brian walked into the store and immediately noticed several boxes in one of the aisles. Remembering his grandfather's story, he walked by and looked at how they were being stacked. Not all the rows were straight and older cans had dust on them. In fact, most of the cans were not even faced out. 'I don't think I would have ever noticed that before.' He walked back to the refrigerator case and grabbed two 16-ounce bottles of water. Trying to decide what to eat, he continued up toward the counter. At the checkout an older teenaged boy stood talking with a couple of boys who looked to be about the same age. "That's bull," he heard the counter help say, "I never said that."

"Well, that's what she's telling everyone," one of the other boys replied.

"Excuse me," Brian said, "how much is a bean and cheese burrito?"

"A buck-fifty," answered the boy, without glancing at Brian. To his friend he said, "If you see her before I do tell her for me she's a damned liar."

Brian looked in the warm case where the burritos were and noticed that one of the shelves had a little mold growing in the corner. Deciding against a burrito he selected a small bag of corn chips and slid the five dollar bill toward the boy with one hand while holding up the two waters and chips with his other. "Huh … three sixty-five. One thirty-five's your change." He counted out the change and pushed the money at Brian, then continued with his friend, "I hope I see her first; I'll straighten her out."

Brian collected his change and started to the door. He opened the door and actually felt good about leaving.

"Chips? Is that the best you could do, Boyo?"

Brian said nothing as he handed his grandfather a bottled water. He just shook his head and fastened his seat belt as Frank prepared to leave. He knew that what he'd just experienced was not uncommon, but after hearing about the Appetitto Shop and good customer service and reading about respect and pride Brian felt the need to think.

Frank saw that something was bothering the boy and thought it best to leave him be. "How about some Beach Boys music kiddo? In my day it was always good on a road trip."

"Sure, Gramps," Brian said brightening up, "that's fine."

On the outskirts of Bend, Frank saw a diner that had a classic rock and roll theme. "We've been listening to the music Brian, what about a burger and a shake?"

Brian smiled and quickly agreed. The restaurant had an old-fashioned jukebox that was playing a Buddy Holly song as they walked in. The place was exceptionally clean with vinyl seats and Formica countertops. Matching booths lined the walls and on each table a small jukebox gave diners the chance to select and pay for songs of their choosing. Frank walked over and sat down in one of these booths. Brian slid into the seat opposite his grandfather and immediately started to flip through the music selections to see what they had. "Love Me Tender ... Jailhouse Rock ... they have a lot of Elvis here. Gramps, did you listen to 'the King' when you were young?"

"Of course, everyone did. Why do think they called him the King? We listened to a lot of different stuff but Elvis always seemed to have a hit on the charts."

"Got a couple of quarters? I want to hear this one." Brian said, indicating 'Jailhouse Rock' and then asked Frank if he saw a song he would like to hear.

"Here you are ... hmm ... do they have 'Johnny Be Good' by Chuck Berry?"

Just then a waitress came over to the table and said, "Johnny Be Good is M4. Hi, I'm Sharon, and I'll be your waitress today. Here are our menus and some waters. I'll be right back to take your order. Our special today is the Buddy Burger with fries, and the soup of the day is chicken noodle. Is there anything I can get for you now?"

Frank looked up and replied, "No, thank you, Sharon, we'd like to look at the menu for a minute."

Brian made the song selections, sat back in his seat and glanced over the menu. "Burger, fries and a shake ... sounds good to me."

"Sounds good to me too, but I can't eat like that anymore. I'll have a burger but with a side salad and a cup of soup."

Sharon came back, took their order, and soon the travelers were enjoying their lunch.

The sounds of 'Jailhouse Rock' filled the restaurant as Brian paused between french fries and waving one at Frank, said, "You know Gramps, this place is okay. I could eat here again. The food is good. I feel comfortable and Sharon took good care of us."

"Glad to hear that. Let me ask you a question then," Frank continued, "would you rather work here or at that mini-mart back there on the road?"

"Definitely here; this place rocks."

"What if I told you that both places offer an equal chance for the staff to honor the customer and themselves?"

"No way, I'd much rather work here."

"You're missing the point, Brian. Obviously, this restaurant is nicer, better designed and well run. It does rock. But the point is, no matter where you work you can do the best job you are capable of ... provide a high level of customer service, and walk away at the end of the day feeling good about the job you've done. You can take pride in any kind of work as long as it's honest work and done to the best of your ability."

"Sure ... okay, whatever."

Frank smiled and changed the subject. "Oh, good here's my song."

They heard the last notes of 'Johnny Be Good' just as they finished their lunch. Brian went to use the bathroom while Frank paid at the register. Outside, he waited at the truck for Brian. When the youngster joined him Frank asked, "Hey Boyo, do you have a driver's license on you?"

"A learner's permit, yeah ... why?"

"'Cause you're driving for a while ... that's the why."

"Really! Sweet! Thanks, Grandpa. I'll be really careful; I promise. It's not hard ... I mean with the camper and boat and all ... is it?"

"Not a'tall." Frank replied with an Irish brogue. Then in a normal voice continued, "Just drive carefully and don't go much above 60 no matter what the speed limit is. Take it easy on turns and let any vehicles that want to pass you, do so." He threw Brian the keys as he spoke and walked over to the passenger side and climbed in.

Brian, feeling somewhat apprehensive but excited at the same time, pulled himself into the driver's seat saying, "I've never driven anything this big before. Dad only lets me drive the old Honda."

"Like a lot of things, once you get used to it it's a piece of cake. By the way, I'll bet you that bathroom was spotless, right?"

"Well ... yeah, how did you know?"

"Just a hunch; it seemed like a well-run place and most people judge the cleanliness of a restaurant by how clean the bathrooms are. I guess the owners know that and make sure their employees are aware of it too."

Juniper trees no bigger than oversized bushes and sagebrush dotted the hillsides. Rimrock laced the small valleys that lined the highway. Brian carefully drove east out of Bend. The change from the lush forest on the west side of the Cascades to the high desert of central Oregon was startling. Brian grinned as he guided the camper and boat along the road. It sure was nice of his grandfather to let him drive, he thought.

Frank watched the boy settle in to driving and smiled as well. Without another word he changed CDs to a '70's Greatest Hits' collection he had, stretched his legs out, took off his glasses, pulled his hat down over his eyes and proceeded to take a nap.

Brian concentrated on his driving. The size of the truck with a camper and boat took a little getting used to. When his grandfather started to sleep, Brian was too surprised and nervous to say anything, but now, feeling more confident, he began to enjoy the drive. There wasn't a lot of traffic, with only an occasional vehicle wanting to pass. Oncoming traffic was light as well. He noticed a small jackrabbit on the side of the road and made a mental note that there wasn't much of a shoulder along this highway. The miles slipped by, as did the time. After about an hour, Brian noticed the terrain seemed rougher and the vegetation grew sparse. 'It isn't all sand dunes like on television, but this is definitely a desert.'

Just as he was about to wake up his grandfather, Brian spotted a deer standing on the side of the highway. He remembered what Frank had said to Delores about it being better to hit a deer rather than lose control of the car and hoped he would not have to deal with that kind of situation. He'd noticed a dead deer lying alongside the road earlier and knew the possibility existed. But this deer just stood there as they passed and Brian felt himself relax. He thought back to their lunch at the diner. He was really enjoying this camping trip so far and the time spent with his grandfather. 'He's kinda cool, for an old man. One thing for sure, he likes to tell stories.'

Something nagged at him about the word 'pride.' When he looked it up in the dictionary, Brian expected to see one thing and found more than he had bargained for; it wasn't all good, either. The variety of definitions and little differences between uses surprised him. He thought that maybe he was missing something that his grandfather was trying to teach him but wasn't sure what it could be. He didn't like feeling uncertain, so he decided to spend a little more time studying the dictionary. He was determined to figure this out. He wanted to impress his grandfather.

When the CD started to repeat itself Brian chose to listen to a few more songs before waking up Frank. 'This old rock and roll isn't half bad,' he thought, 'and since my iPod was gone it's better than nothing.'

In the middle of a song, Brian decided to wake up Frank. He turned up the volume just as the chorus started up, "I just want to celebrate … another day of living …" and when his grandfather sat up and joined in, "I just want to celebrate another day of life ..." he knew his timing was good.

"Good nap?"

"Yes Brian, it was. How's driving?"

"Piece of cake, just like you said."

"Where are we?"

"I'm not exactly sure, about halfway ... I think."

Frank laughed and made a sound like blaring horn, "Aaaghh! Wrong answer. Where are we?"

"Central Oregon?"

"Aaaghh! Wrong again. We are HERE! That is where we are; here. What time is it?" he asked turning in his seat to face his grandson.

Brian smiled, knowing his grandfather was playing with him. "About two-thirty I'd guess."

"Aaaghh! Wrong answer. What time is it?"

Brian thought about it for a minute, and hesitated as he replied, "Now?"

"Very good. That's right; it is now. Here and now. So many times we forget the here and now. We get caught up in the past or the future without realizing that all we really have is the here and now." Frank spoke with an increasing excitement, "We ... ahem, we are driving ... together ... on a perfect summer's day, driving, I say ... toward our next campsite ... where we will ... I promise, catch some trout."

Brian laughed at the delivery of his grandfather's little sermon. "Amen, brother ... say amen!" he added, waving one hand in the air.

"Amen."

Chapter Eleven

On the map Chickahominy Reservoir resembled a tiny, slightly bent index finger whose tip rested on the north side of Highway 20, just west of a red dot named Riley. Riley in turn lay 20 or so miles west of Burns. A small red tepee meant a Bureau of Land Management campground awaited any travelers who might want to stay. The campground at Chickahominy Reservoir was unlike any that Brian could imagine. It was barren and rocky; if not for the signs, the toilet facilities, a fish cleaning station and a boat ramp, the area resembled a campground one might expect to see on the moon.

As Brian pulled into a campsite, a strong, dry wind out of the southwest blasted stinging sand across the desolate landscape. Right in front of them it created a dust devil, a tornado in miniature that swirled from the campground to a few small hills that lay beyond. There were no trees. Broken ground disrupted only by a few sage and juniper bushes surrounded the campground and reservoir. The wind rocked the camper and boat. Even after Frank had turned off the truck and set the brake, it still felt as if they were doing a decent pace on the highway.

"This is some wind, huh, Gramps?"

"It sure is. I hope it dies down soon so we can fish some this evening. I don't see anyone out fishing right now."

"I don't see anyone out at all," Brian replied. "Who would want to be out in this?"

"Nobody in his right mind, Brian, but we are talking about fishermen. The first condition is not necessarily a prerequisite for the other."

"Well, I sure wouldn't want to be out there if I could help it."

"A wise and prudent boy, an excellent boy … this wind should drop in a while. In the meantime, let's unhitch the boat and start to set up camp. Once we get the camper cleared out we can hang out inside until it settles down."

"We're not going out there right now, are we?"

"No, I suppose we can wait. What do you want to talk about now? You were telling me about school?" Frank replied, referring to an earlier discussion.

"There isn't much more to tell," Brian shrugged. "I'll tell you what though; I'm amazed at the change in the climate and trees between the North Umpqua and here. This is desert."

"Do you want to know why?"

"Sure."

"Prevailing winds coming in from the Pacific Ocean carry clouds heavy with moisture. First, they encounter the Coast Range of mountains and then the Cascades, each time dropping rain. Only the biggest storms retain enough moisture to rain over here, resulting in rainforest west of the Cascades, desert on the east side."

"So, we went from rainforest at Whitehorse Falls to desert in what, 50 miles or less?" asked Brian.

"Yep, that's correct."

"Wow!" Brian paused, and remembering something he had thought of earlier, continued, "Okay, then, tell me about fly fishing. I've only been fishing a couple of times and I wouldn't mind learning how."

"I've got a couple of magazines and a how-to book in the camper. Read those tonight. They'll provide you with some background and tomorrow we'll give it a try. This evening, after we set up camp we'll get the boat in the water and try our hand at trolling for trout or find a likely looking spot to fish our way through."

"Sounds fine, Gramps."

"Whenever you go about learning a new skill there is a trick I learned at the Appetitto Shop that will help. Want to know what it is?"

"Well ... yeah." Brian said with a smile and tone that expressed willingness.

"All right then, it comes with a story."

"What a shock ... there's a story involved." Brian laughed.

"Smart aleck," Frank said joining in the laughter. "I'll try to make it short, okay? Okay; one day after I'd been working behind the counter for a week or so, I became aware that Tony was watching me make a sandwich. When I finished the customer left and we had a little lull. He said, Frank, I want to talk to you about how to learn a new skill. This applies to anything you want to learn, but today we're going to use making a sandwich as an example. I said okay, and he continued, whenever you learn something new you go through four stages of learning: explanation, demonstration, imitation and repetition. If you learn the skill correctly and practice it correctly, you may achieve mastery."

"For example, when you first made a sandwich, you were really careful about each step. At this point, I thought Tony was trying to tell me I wasn't being careful, so I began to tell him that I was always careful. He stopped me short. He said, son I want you to listen to what I'm really trying to say ... I'm not criticizing you. I am using this as an example. Let me finish. Okay then, there is a critical element in each step that can lead to excellence. You know Brian, he said, 'can lead to excellence,' and it took me years to figure out what he was trying to say."

Frank paused to take a swig of water. "I'm getting sidetracked. I do this sometimes. Let me explain and then I'll get back to the story. Tony was trying to say that excellence is an ongoing process. I figured that out eventually, but at the time I was just interested in hearing about the stages of learning. Tony often taught more than one lesson at the same time. I just didn't get it then."

"Anyway, he picked up a loaf of hero bread and a knife and continued, when you are shown a skill for the first time, your teacher should explain the skill. In the next stage the instructor demonstrates the proper technique. If you learn the wrong way to do something you'll never get to be really good at it. Make sense? I said it did and he smiled. In the third stage, imitation, the critical element is correct practice. This is where a good coach comes in handy."

"The fourth stage, repetition, you practice the skill over and over until it becomes automatic. If you think about it, study it and work toward making little improvements, eventually you'll become really good at it. You compare how you do it to the ideal way to do it. I'm talking about excellence here, he said. I nodded yes. Tony put the bread on the counter and with one sure cut sliced into the bread. I remembered the first time he showed me how to make a sandwich; he cut the bread the same way. Notice how when I slice the bread, he said, I place my hand on top; see how I draw the knife in one smooth motion. My fingers are safe from being cut and when I'm done the bread is in the correct hand for the next step. There is no wasted motion. Every part of making a sandwich can be studied the same way: slicing and stacking the meat, positioning the cheese, adding the other stuff and wrapping it up ... oh, and presenting it to the customer. Each of these little skills can be improved upon until you have become really good at each one. When each skill is perfected you put them all together. This can lead to mastery. When he finished, he paused and said with emphasis, this goes for anything you are learning."

"I thought then about my sandwich making skills and realized I didn't cut the bread that well. And for the others parts, well, I could improve those areas too. Then ... suddenly, I understood Tony was saying more to me. I wanted to know more about mastery. I said okay, Tony what's critical beyond the last stage? He smiled and kind of slapped me on the shoulder and replied … Great question! I'm glad you thought about that. The answer lies within you after you get past repetition. I can't answer that for you."

"Did you ever figure it out, Gramps?"

"Eventually, I did, yes."

"What is it?"

"It's something you have to learn for yourself. I can't answer that for you."

"Thanks a lot … Yoda."

Frank laughed and felt relieved Brian was interested. He liked the boy's sense of humor and his reference to one of Frank's favorite fictional characters. He replied in a raspy voice, "Curious you are, but not until you are ready, will you discover the true nature of the Force."

It was Brian's turn to laugh.

The wind finally died down. Frank looked at his watch. "Brian, we better get a move on if we want to get everything done. Help me unhitch the boat and let's get the camper ready."

"Sure enough, Gramps."

Shortly thereafter, the boat sat on its trailer to one side of the camper. The extra gear that had been inside the boat and in the camper lay neatly stacked under a tarp. Frank paused and considered the campsite. "Brian, normally I'd set the jacks on the camper, pull the truck out and hitch the boat trailer back up to it. Then, we'd back it down the boat ramp into the water, but since it is such a small, light boat I think it would be faster if we just carried it down there and made a few trips with the poles and stuff. Okay?"

"Anything to save some time, Gramps; I really want to get fishing."

As they were preparing to carry the boat the short distance to the reservoir, the occupants of the trailer in the campsite next to them pulled up in their pickup truck. An elderly man got out from behind the driver's seat and walked over to Frank and Brian. A short woman of about the same age got out and went directly to the trailer. "Hi there, guys, I guess we're neighbors in this wasteland." Offering his hand he continued, "My name is Pete Smith and that there is my wife Fanny. See you're getting ready to do some fishing."

Frank shook the man's hand and replied, "That we are, Pete. I'm Frank and this is my grandson, Brian. Any suggestions on what the trout might be bitin'?"

"Worms and cheese always work well enough for me. I don't bother with all that fancy gear."

Frank smiled and said, "Thanks for the tip. Well then, we better get going; the boy here wants to get his line wet."

"You're not fixing to carry that thing, are you? They do have a boat ramp you know." Pete added in a somewhat superior manner, "It's a lot easier to back the boat down that way."

"Oh, I know, but we figured this would be quicker, and besides it's not a heavy boat. We'll be fine. But thank you for your advice." Frank nodded at Brian. "Ready, Boyo, one, two, three ... go."

Pete looked surprised Frank didn't heed his advice. "Suit yourself," he said and without another word the elderly man turned his back and walked toward his trailer.

They quickly slid the boat into the water. Frank tied it up to a small pier and told Brian to fetch the poles, the oars and a tackle box they had left back at the camper. "I'll get this little trolling motor set up," he said, "while you make a couple of trips getting the gear. Don't forget the life vests."

They were about to get underway when Brian asked Frank about their conversation with Pete. "Gramps, that old man seemed kind of irritated. Did we do something to bother him?"

"No Brian, some people develop a way they do things or get in the habit of thinking a certain way. They become so attached to their way, they believe it's the only way. Anything new or different makes them uncomfortable. They generally have real strong ideas about how things ... should be." Frank stressed the words, 'should be' adding, "When these people encounter something different they generally don't have anything nice to say. I believe if you don't have something nice to say, it's better not to say anything at all."

"I've heard my dad say that before. He must have learned it from you."

"What a pleasant thought that is. My son may have actually learned something from me after all. More'n likely it's from a Disney movie," Frank replied with sarcasm.

Brian was surprised by his grandfather's tone. "You know Gramps, I've heard that you and my dad had some sort of a fight and for a while you guys weren't even talking to each other. What's that all about?"

"Well, Brian it's a long story ... maybe some other time. Right now we should get this thing going. I'm going to steer using this little motor. You sit up front and be careful not to lean too far over the side. I don't want to go for a swim."

"Okay, Gramps."

"When we get a little farther out into the reservoir we'll set you up to catch some fish."

The small boat cut through the water, leaving a tiny wake. The gentle rolling of the boat combined with the warm summer breeze might have felt relaxing to Brian if he wasn't so excited to be out in a boat, fishing. He sat on the seat in the bow gazing ahead, wondering how many fish swam under the surface of the water.

They had not gone more than 200 yards when Frank turned the motor off. Reaching for a tackle box he said to Brian, "Hand me that black pole there son, and I'll show you how to set up your line. Let's see, I think we'll try this blue and silver Rooster-tail with a slow troll and see if we can get a trout to strike. I'll use this green

Chickahominy Reservoir

Flat-fish to see if it works." In a way that allowed Brian to watch, Frank tied the lures slowly and deliberately to a set-up on each pole. When he was done he handed the black pole back to Brian. Now, Brian do you know how to let out line and reel in?"

"Like this?" asked Brian as he demonstrated first letting out the line and then reeling in.

"Exactly. Okay then, I'll start up the motor and when we're fully under way, let out enough line so that you're fishing about 20 or so yards behind the boat. You fish the right side of the boat, or the starboard side, as it's known in boating lingo, and I'll fish the port side. That way our lines should not get tangled. I'm going to make a series of gradual turns that will serve to change speeds and the depth of the lures and if we're lucky, we'll get a big trout to strike. If you feel a fish, yell 'Fish on' and I'll reel in and help you land it. If I get a 'fish on' we switch roles. Okay?"

"Got it. Is that what the net is for?"

"Yep, that's right. If these don't work I've got some other lures we can try. Sometimes though, the fish just aren't biting. It's really just a combination of luck, preparation and skill … mostly luck."

They had fished for about 20 minutes without any action. The early evening sky, cloudless and featuring a fat crescent moon, began to take on a bright turquoise color. Frank had trolled along the east side of the reservoir, heading in a northerly direction and had just decided to change lures when Brian's pole suddenly bent.

"Fish on … fish on!" he said loudly. "I've got one Gramps! I've got one!" Brian was plainly excited.

As Frank reeled in he spoke to Brian in a calm, matter-of-fact voice. "All right, Boyo, if he wants to take some line, let him … when you feel some slack in the line, reel in. You want to keep steady pressure on the fish so it can't get off or go on a sudden run and snap the line."

Brian fought the trout for a few minutes. He had gotten the fish near the boat once, but then it went on a long run and had taken quite a bit of line.

As the line peeled off the reel, Frank whistled. "This must be a pretty big trout, Brian, for it to take that much line. I've got the drag on the reel set for around five pounds. Oh! And the line is light. You must play this size fish correctly or it'll be gone. Keep playin' it, Boyo ... you're doin' fine."

After another shorter run, Brian finally brought the fish close enough to the boat for Frank to get a look at it. "Whoa, Brian this is a monster. I'll bet it's 18 inches long and weighs three pounds. Take your time now," he said excitedly, "don't let it use the boat to get off. If you can, hold your pole up and try to guide the fish over here where I can net it."

Brian didn't reply but held the pole up and tried to bring the trout near his grandfather. He laughed occasionally but said nothing as he concentrated on landing the trout.

Frank glanced at his grandson and recognized the look of joy that accompanies catching such a fish. He smiled and thought, 'If he wasn't one before, Brian is going to be a fisherman now.'

Brian felt the strength of the fish through the line as it struggled against the hook. Finally the trout stopped struggling and Brian guided it over to his grandfather. As Frank slipped the net around the big trout, Brian remembered to breathe. His grandfather held the net up, the big trout still struggling inside. Brian yelled, "Yeah! What a fish ... what a fight."

His grandfather smiled at Brian, reached into the net, slid his fingers under the trout's gill and held it up. "This is a beauty, Boyo. It's at least three pounds. Tonight we eat well." Brian watched Frank reach under his seat and retrieve a small wooden club. With it, his grandfather struck the fish sharply on the head. Then, using a small set of pliers, he removed the hook from the fish. "Okay … great fish, Brian. What a way to get started."

Drifting into a nearby inlet, Frank dropped a small anchor and declared, "Okay, now we'll try our luck casting flies. If we catch any more fish using these," Frank said as he pulled out some flies from a small container and held them up, "it will be a lot easier to release them. They have barbless hooks."

They changed set-ups and proceeded to cast flies using clear bobbers that held a small amount of water for weight. A short leader ran from the bobbers to the flies. Frank explained, "We're really casting the bobber and the fly is just along for the ride. In a lot of instances this is a viable alternative to fly fishing. At least," he added, "using these flies we'll be able to release any other fish we catch. What with the fish you already caught, we've got more than enough trout for dinner, and breakfast, for that matter."

Brian smiled with pride as his grandfather spoke those last words. His focus suddenly changed as he felt a sudden pull on his line. "Fish on! I've got another one, Gramps."

"Well, so do I! Fish on! Let's try to keep them apart and land them both; mine doesn't seem too big."

The trout on Brian's line didn't seem to be as big either. Frank quickly and easily brought his fish up to the boat. He reached down to tilt the hook. This released the fish without Frank having to touch it. Soon Brian's second catch swam free as well.

Frank declared the day a success. "Well Boyo, we caught some fish, had some fun, and we'll have trout for dinner … all in all, a good day, huh? It's time to get back so we can get dinner and prepare for tomorrow." Brian quickly agreed and reeled in his line. Within minutes they were on the way back in.

Chapter Twelve

The small trolling motor made little progress against a steady wind and not until the sun began to cast a dull, red glow low along the western horizon did Frank and Brian finally tie up at the pier. As Brian carried the fishing poles and other gear up to the camper, Frank secured the boat. He knew they would be up early to fish, so he used the last remaining daylight to rearrange the small craft. He wanted to be as prepared as possible.

Brian carried a flashlight down to his grandfather. "Hey, old man … it's getting dark. Do you need some help, or can I just shed some light on the subject for you?"

"I was just done, Brian, but thank you. I always did enjoy a good light-shedding; I don't mind the company either."

"The trout is in this cooler, right?"

"That's right. Before we get dinner ready, we should get a picture of you and the fish. We need evidence of your monster trout or no one will believe us."

"I guess. Isn't it too dark?"

"Not at all, you get the lantern on and I'll turn on the camper's little porch light. With that, and the flash from the camera, we should have enough light to get a good enough picture."

"Okay, Gramps." Brian stood holding his trout. "How should I hold it?"

"Slip a couple of your fingers through the gill, and hold it up." Frank placed Brian with his catch in front of the door of the camper. Light from the lantern helped illuminate the proud boy with his catch. Frank continued, "Okay, Brian, hold it a little more in front of you, closer to the camera; it will make the fish look even bigger."

"Isn't that cheating, Gramps?"

"Not a'tall, Boyo ... simply good storytelling. When we're done we can go down to the fish cleaning station and gut it."

Back in the camper, Brian sat at the table while Frank stood in front of the stove cooking. The only light came from a small LED wall light and a small lantern. He filled a measuring cup with water and after he poured it into a three-quart pot, he read aloud the directions from a package of rice and beans. "Bring two cups water to a boil; add spice packet and oil before adding contents. By George, I think I've got it." He turned to smile at Brian, and then continued, "Would you like to learn a little bit of cooking? It'll serve you well some day, I promise."

"Sure Gramps. What's next?"

"Hmm ... what is next ... Let's see, I suppose we should get the trout ready while we're waiting for the water to boil. The salad is in a plastic bag in the cooler, and I thought we might enjoy a little soup, too."

"Sounds good to me; I'm starving."

"Good, then I guess it's time for you to fillet your fish."

"Fillet the fish? I don't know how, Gramps. Could you show me?"

"WHY SOITENLY! I'll fillet one side and you do the other."

Frank proceeded to describe, step by step, the way he filleted a fish. He deliberately matched his actions to his instructions.

Brian traded places with his grandfather and started to fillet the second side; he felt nervous but eager. "Is this right?" he asked.

"That's right ... now slide the knife along the bone." Frank kept up a constant stream of instructions and encouragement. "Yep, if you keep the blade at a sharper angle ... exactly," and as Brian finished, added, "Good job, well done."

The large trout now lay in two fat fillets on the cutting board. Frank collected the head, tail and skeleton of the big fish and swept them into a plastic bag along with the packaging from the rice. "We'll save half of this guy for another time ... no need to cook more than we're ready to eat, maybe for breakfast. There is nothing quite like fresh trout and eggs."

Not completely convinced, Brian replied, "Really."

"Yeah, really," answered his grandfather with a grin.

Steam from the pot of water caught Frank's attention. "It looks like we can add the other stuff and the rice. It says here to stir occasionally. Here's a spoon. That's your job while I show you the proper way to fry this."

Brian accepted the spoon, stirred the rice and beans twice and paid close attention to his grandfather. He noticed Frank wrap up one of the fillets and place it in the refrigerator. Then, from the inside door of the refrigerator, he retrieved a stick of butter.

"You'll need a little butter, some shallots or green onions, seasoned breadcrumbs, spices, salt, pepper and a little white wine if you have it." Pulling a frying pan from one of the cabinets, Frank placed it on the stove. From the cabinet above the sink he retrieved a bottle of wine. "A nice chardonnay ... since we need some to cook with, I suppose I'll just have to drink a glass with dinner." Frank spoke in a slow voice that conveyed resignation; however, his smile convinced Brian that having a chardonnay with dinner wouldn't be much of a sacrifice for his grandfather.

A lit match helped ignite the gas stovetop. Another search of the refrigerator produced chopped shallots. The spices were kept handy in a wooden rack attached to the wall behind the stove. Cutting the second fillet into two pieces, Frank dusted each piece with breadcrumbs. Melting butter sizzled as the fish joined the shallots in the pan. Quickly, Frank produced another pot and opened a can of soup. He poured the soup into the pot and turned to Brian. "Give that an occasional stir too, my boy."

Brian laughed, suddenly reminded of his job; he stirred first the rice, then the soup.

Frank opened the cabinet over the stove, reached up and said, "If we had time I would have made us some fresh biscuits, but these will have to do for tonight." He held up a package of store-bought biscuits. "Now I'll add the spices and the wine, turn the fish and get our china and silverware ready." He placed two paper plates, a couple of plastic bowls and utensils on the table.

The aroma of the various dishes filled the camper. The steam from the cooking fogged up the windows and the heat from the stove warmed the camper. It felt cozy. Brian's mouth watered as Frank dished up their dinner. Soon, the only sounds heard were those of utensils clinking and an occasional sigh of satisfaction from one of the diners.

"That was great, Gramps," Brian spoke first. "Everything was just delicious."

"I'm glad you enjoyed it, Brian. It was an honor to serve you."

"Well, you did yourself proud. Hey, that's something else my dad always says ... you did yourself proud. I'll bet he got that expression from you too, huh, Gramps?"

"Yes, I believe he may well have picked that up from me. I use that quite regularly. Maybe he did learn something from me after all."

"You know, Grandpa, I've been thinking about something you said earlier about my dad saying, 'If you can't say something nice don't say anything at all.' And even if he did hear it from a movie, I'm sure he also heard it from you. Wouldn't that sort of show your influence?"

Frank paused to reflect on Brian's question. Finally he responded, "You're absolutely right. Maybe I've been a little harsh in my judgment of him."

"Okay, Gramps, what's the story on all this?"

"Well, Brian, it's a long story. The short version is that your grandmother and I met right out of high school. We fell in love, got married and started a family. So far, so good. However, Moira had started smoking cigarettes when she was 14. There was little evidence in those days to suggest the danger of cancer associated with smoking. I never did think it was a good thing, so I wanted her to quit. She tried a number of times but could never kick the habit." Frank paused, cleared his throat and continued, "Smoking and the addiction to nicotine is a powerful habit. Even after the evidence began to grow linking smoking with cancer she just couldn't quit … she died at 49. She was too young to die, but … die she did, leaving me with two teenaged kids and an emptiness that I've never been entirely able to get over."

"I threw myself into work and I became hard to live with. The kids, your dad and your Aunt Mary, went through a tough time as well. They had lost their mother to cancer, and their father to grief. I was there all right; in the house. But I know now that I wasn't really available to either of them. They needed their father to be there and I was too caught up in my own grief. Eventually, I was able to gain some perspective. I realized that life was much too precious to continue to live the way I had been living. I made a commitment to myself and to my children to go through life being a positive influence to those around me. As I started out on this new way … this new way of living, I was hard on myself and I was hard on the kids, particularly your father. It was about this time that I discovered that Robert had started smoking cigarettes. I went ballistic." Frank stopped, looked at Brian and wiped his face with a paper towel.

"It was one thing to start smoking before all the evidence linking smoking with cancer was available and quite another to start when so much information existed, and especially after his mother died from cancer caused by smoking. The harder I pushed, the more he dug in his heels and refused to give up smoking. It became the only thing we fought about because it was the only thing I would talk to him about. I wish I had been more patient and understanding. Maybe if I had been I would have had more influence with him. I don't know, maybe then we could have had a better relationship and maybe then he would have quit smoking."

"Dad did quit, Grandpa. He quit smoking a couple of years ago. Didn't he tell you?"

Frank heard the words but a long moment went by before he could bring himself to speak. "He did? That's great news. No, since my last visit with your family it has never come up. I swore I'd never fight with him again about smoking and without that we seemed to have normal conversations for a change. This, this … is wonderful news. I'm glad he stopped."

"He never told you he quit?"

"No, after all the fights we had we both kinda walked on eggshells, so to speak. I guess he made the decision to quit on his own." But Frank wondered, 'Why wouldn't Robert tell me he quit?'

Brian shook his head in disbelief. "So, you guys fought over the same thing for years." Pausing, he continued in a doubtful tone of voice, "I have seen my father when he decides to be stubborn about something but I didn't realize stubbornness was hereditary."

Frank let his grandson's words sink in. He looked at Brian and responded with a deep laugh. "You're absolutely right, Brian, I can't blame him for being stubborn; after all, the fruit doesn't fall far from the tree. So, are you stubborn too?"

Brian looked at his grandfather, smiled and said in an Irish brogue, "Me? Not a'tall."

Chapter Thirteen

The alarm, set for five o'clock in the morning, sounded louder in the camper than the alarm clock Brian used back home, yet seemed less obnoxious. He looked forward to another day of fishing and quickly got out of his sleeping bag. Today he would try his hand at fly fishing. After dinner last night his grandfather had shown him the fly fishing equipment, demonstrated two of the most common knots and had Brian practice tying them. According to Frank, fly fishing took skill, patience and most of all ... luck. After Brian read a few magazine articles his grandfather had in the camper and skimmed through an old, well-worn book on the subject, he thought he had a pretty good idea of what to do. His grandfather had reminded him often before they went to sleep that catching a big trout was a rare event and catching any trout with a fly was an accomplishment; the sport was in presenting the right fly in just the right way to tempt a fish to strike.

Frank, in the meantime, swung his legs out of his bed and reached across the narrow aisle of the camper to turn off the alarm clock. He flipped on a small battery-powered lantern and smiled when he saw that Brian was already getting down from the bunk.

"Good morning, Brian. I guess you want to go fishing, huh?"

"You bet, Gramps. I can't wait."

"Well, we need to get our beds put up and have a little breakfast. There's no need to rush out there since we have some fly fishing practice to do and we'll need full daylight for that."

"Okay, Gramps, whatever you say."

When Brian stepped out of the camper to walk to the outhouse, the darkness was softening with a golden glow on the eastern horizon. Above this, a faint band of blue sky melted into the blackness where some of the night's stars still twinkled. There was no wind and the only sound was birdsong. Brian couldn't identify which kind of bird proclaimed the new day but decided it sounded somehow triumphant. The strong scent of sage and juniper assailed his nostrils. He stood still for awhile and breathed deeply, aware of it all.

"Whoa ..." he exclaimed under his breath, "too cool!"

Crunching loose rock and gravel with every step, he walked slowly toward the outhouse. Even though the camper had a toilet, Frank requested that as long as they had public facilities available, they use them to conserve both the camper's water and waste storage capacity for when the whole family joined them.

Frank had told him, "The girls will need to use the bathroom more than us guys anyway," and Brian had to admit that, as usual, his grandfather made sense. Brian was impressed with his grandfather. Frank almost always knew what he was doing and why. He appeared to think about things and come up with just the right alternative whenever he had to make a decision. More than once, Brian noticed this about his grandfather and was both impressed and curious about how he did it.

The outhouse smelled really bad and as soon as Brian was outside again he closed the door behind him and took a deep breath. Cool, clean, fresh air perfumed with juniper filled his lungs and brought a smile. The glow in the east had grown, and the sky above was now more blue than black. A handful of stars sprinkled in the west continued to be visible but dawn was certainly ... now. All around him Brian could see the landscape better. The day's first sunlight peeked over the horizon just as Brian reached the camper.

"Hey, Gramps, the sun's coming up and it's a beautiful morning. Let's get fishin'."

"All in good time, my boy," Frank said with a chuckle, "all in good time. First, how about a little breakfast? You know it is the most important meal of the day."

"I've heard that before. Is it true?"

"I believe it is. When you get home, if you want to research it, I'll bet you'll come up with a reliable answer."

Brian replied, "I might just do that."

"In the meantime, I've got trout and eggs, coffee, juice and leftover biscuits all ready for us. There's butter and honey," Frank said, pointing, "for the biscuits. That should tide us over till lunch and if we end up fishing into the afternoon I've got some snacks, jerky and dried fruit, and some soft drinks all packed and ready to go."

"Sounds great, Gramps; I am actually kind of hungry."

After eating and cleaning up after breakfast, Frank collected the gear, loaded down his grandson with some of it, and led him down to the boat. Moving quickly, he set a brisk pace. Brian shuffled his feet more than once just to keep up. He grinned at his grandfather's apparent excitement. Brian's enthusiasm grew with every step.

Frank reached the small boat first and placed one of the bags he carried on the pier next to the boat. He turned to Brian and said, "Hey, Boyo, unload that gear—" Frank said pointing to the bucket Brian held in his left hand, "—into the stern of the boat, that's the back, you know … the rest here," pointing to a spot next to the bag, "and go back for the cooler, okay?"

"Sure Gramps. No problem."

Brian hurried back with the cooler. By the time he reached the boat Frank had distributed the remaining gear and sat in the boat on the bench nearest to the stern and the trolling motor.

"Okay then, carefully slide the cooler onto the seat in the middle, while I hold onto this cleat. You untie the rope tied to that cleat," Frank pointed to a small metal prong to which the boat was still tied, "and then carefully step in."

Without answer Brian did as he was told but almost lost his balance as he stepped into the small boat. Frank held on to the cleat

Fly Fishing

and shifted his weight to help keep the boat somewhat steady, but Brian fell down onto the seat rather clumsily.

"Whoa, there Boyo ... steady now. You almost went for a swim."

"I sure ... did." stammered Brian, "I didn't expect it to rock like that."

"It helps to step into the exact center of this little skiff and steady yourself with your hand to keep your balance. You'll catch on soon, I'm sure." Frank paused and laughed, adding, "If you don't, I assume you know how to swim, right?"

"Yeah, very funny; I can swim but I'd rather wait till I have a bathing suit on."

Frank pulled away from the pier and headed north toward the main section of Chickahominy Reservoir.

"We'll head to a cove on the east side of the lake, Brian."

"That's cool, Gramps. I can't wait."

As the small boat made steady progress toward their goal, Frank continued to look ahead while making a series of small adjustments. Tiny waves from a soft wind rippled the surface of the reservoir. A cloudless blue sky promised a beautiful day. Brian felt curious about why Frank chose that particular place to start fishing.

"What made you decide to fish there first, Gramps?"

"Well, Brian ... really, I guess one place is as good as another, but since I'm going to show you how to cast a fly, I wanted a shore with a lot of clear space behind us to avoid tangles with trees or brush, and with the wind in our faces and the sun at our back. This cove," Frank said nodding toward the place they were headed "fits the bill perfectly."

"Makes sense, I guess." Brian answered. "But why with the wind in our face?"

"Oh, it'll make controlling your cast a little easier. The wind will hold up the fly as it's about to land on the water and to a trout it might look as if it's a real fly landing on the surface."

"I see. Gee, Gramps you seem to think of everything."

"No Brian, far from it, but I've done this sort of thing before. That's one really good reason to have a more experienced person along to show you the ropes; a guide so to speak, or a coach, to explain what to do and show you the right way to do it. A coach will watch you to see that you do it correctly or help you make adjustments if they are needed. It's like trying to achieve any goal, really."

Frank paused. He thought about it a while then added, "It's like me steering this boat. We have a goal; that cove over there. I aim the boat directly at it, but whatever current or wind is present pushes us slightly off course. If we don't notice this change we won't end up where we want to go. We must keep our eyes or our focus on the goal and when we see we're getting off course, well then, we make a slight change, an adjustment, to direct the boat back to going where we wanted to go in the first place."

"Life is like this too; setting any goal and working toward its completion takes constant evaluation and many adjustments before you can reach your goal. Any job that needs planning, where doing one thing before you can start on the next part is just like that too; one thing at a time ... one step at a time. Just knowing the right thing to do next can be more important than how fast you work. That's something that Tony used to say. He'd say working in the Appetitto Shop wasn't rocket science; there was no one task so hard or complicated that anyone couldn't learn how to do it. The real skill was in looking around and recognizing exactly which job was the most important job to do first. That was the real skill ... knowing what was the most important thing, whatever that was, and getting right on it. He'd say, ask yourself this question, what is the best thing that I can do right now? Now, the answer might be to take some action that moves you closer to your goal, or ask someone for help, or get some rest, or it may be to go fishing, but whatever the answer is, be honest with yourself; be true to yourself and do it. If you follow your heart you generally end up doing okay."

Frank fell silent and Brian took to watching the bow of the boat slice through the water. Sunlight, sparkling like thousands of tiny jewels, danced off the surface of the reservoir while the turbulence created by the passage of the boat seemed to Brian to pulse with its own rhythm. His thoughts were interrupted when suddenly, off to his right, a large trout jumped out of the water and landed with a splash.

"Wow! Gramps, did you see that?"

"Yep. Nice fish. This might be a good spot to start out."

"I'll say. What made him jump like that?"

"Well, it could be it was going after a smaller fish, or maybe a fly, or a hatching insect, or . . . it might be just trying to get a good look at us."

"Yeah, right." Brian answered back with a laugh.

As the boat approached the shore, Frank straightened out the small craft to run up onto the beach. He then cut the motor and pushed down on its handle, which brought the small propeller out of the water.

"Hold on, Brian, we're going to feel a pretty good bump."

"Gramps, what are you doing?"

"Just hold on . . . now."

At that moment the small boat pushed onto the shore, moved up a foot or so and came to an abrupt stop. Frank laughed at the wide-eyed look Brian shot at him and explained, "There's no pier over here, Boyo, and that's the best way to beach a small craft. Now I'll use one of these oars to push us up on shore a little farther. Sit tight for just a minute, won't you?"

Frank reached over and loosened an oar that had been wedged along the gunwale. He swung the oar over his head and planted the paddle end into the sand at the stern. In a fluid motion Frank braced himself against the bench in front of him and pushed hard on the oar. The small craft moved another foot up onto the beach.

"Okay, now Brian, step out carefully onto the beach. I'll use this oar to steady us while you get out and then grab a hold of the bow and pull the boat up a little more."

Brian started to do as he was told but slipped slightly getting out of the boat and planted his right foot in the water. Shaking his foot, he reached over and pulled the boat. It moved easily, which startled Brian until he noticed that his grandfather was still pushing on the oar.

"There we go, Boyo, good job ... now hold onto the boat while I get out. Okay?"

"Sure thing, Gramps."

Frank carefully made his way forward and with Brian steadying the boat was able to step out onto the beach as well. With a chuckle he said, "That was done slick, eh? And I didn't have to get my feet wet either."

"I wasn't so lucky. Heh! You knew my feet could get wet ... didn't you?"

"Age has its privileges, Boyo. It'll dry out soon enough. Besides, you'll want to take your shoes off to fish anyhow. Now grab the other side of the boat like this and we'll pull it up some more."

Brian grinned at his grandfather as they worked together to beach the skiff. Once it was more than halfway up on the shore Frank said, "That'll do Brian, that's good. Let's get the fishing rods and the other gear out and we'll have our first fly fishing lesson."

"Yeah, but first let me take off my shoes and socks."

"Take your time son, take your time."

Chapter Fourteen

Frank's second cast landed just where he wanted it to. Since changing from a dry-fly set-up that had not produced a single bite, he'd gone to a blue-gray nymph, a fly tied to resemble an insect in the larval stage. He waited to see if a nearby trout found this appealing before starting a slow retrieval. Frank looked up to check on Brian, but there was no action on the other side of the small cove either. After he showed his grandson the basics of fly fishing and watched him fish for a short while, they had a small snack of jerky, dried fruit and some tea. Frank then moved northward along the shore till he found a nice spot to fish from. The morning sun warmed his skin and a soft breeze felt refreshing. He looked at the sun rising higher in the sky. It wouldn't be long before it became hot. He had the sunblock along and this led him to smile. Early in his marriage he had been asked repeatedly by his wife if he'd remembered the sunblock, to which he'd replied of course I did and, of course, he hadn't. He'd lived with endless jokes about that and the resulting sunburns for many years. The thought of it brought back to him the realization of his loss. He would never hear those jokes again.

He watched Brian begin the ten o'clock to two o'clock motion used to cast. He let out more line with each forward motion until he finally had enough line to cast. His cast was smooth. 'The boy's arm seems a little stiff, but otherwise, he's doing fine. He needs to learn to let the rod do the work. Well,' Frank thought, 'he's getting the hang of the cast okay; hope he gets a hit soon; it's no fun fishin' without some kind of action.'

The thought occurred to him that if the fish weren't interested in dry flies he ought to tell Brian to switch to a wet set-up as he had, but decided to wait a while to see if his new selection produced any action. In the meantime, he was content. He felt happy just to be alive and fishing with his grandson on such a nice day. The water in front of him rippled as a small trout rolled near the surface. Frank thought, 'Now that's a good sign, it could mean there's a hatch of insect larvae taking place; if we have a fly to match the hatch we could sure have a lot of fun.'

"Hey, Boyo," he called over, "switch to a wet set-up and try that Golden Brown Mayfly nymph. Okay?"

"Sure, Gramps," Brian yelled back as he reeled in, "I'm not doing any good with this, that's for sure."

Nothing in his voice indicated Brian was getting bored or not having a good time but Frank knew that fishing at length without some hits could be tedious. A final glance at the boy made him smile. Brian stood along the bare shoreline carefully tying a new leader onto his line. He seemed totally immersed in the task at hand and Frank thought back to his own youth and the first time his own grandfather had taken him surf casting off Rockaway's beach for striped bass. Frank didn't catch one that first time out, but still had fun. He reflected, 'Sometimes the fun is as much in the effort as in the result.'

From what Brian had read, he knew that it was important when fly fishing to use the right fly. He had been thinking of changing set-ups but didn't feel sure of what to change to until his grandfather called over to him. Yeah, a wet fly made sense; the leader would sink, not float on the surface, so the fly trailing behind it would sink and look like an emerging insect. He felt grateful for the suggestion. As he concentrated on tying the blood-knot that his grandfather had taught him to match the new leader to his line, Brian's tongue stuck out slightly and he constantly rolled it around the corner of his mouth. Once the knot was done he opened a small case that held a variety of flies and selected one he felt sure was the Golden Brown

Mayfly nymph. 'Tie this to the tip of the leader and I'm back in business.'

Brian moved into knee-high water. He used the back and forth motion to let out line. He still repeated to himself the ten o'clock-two o'clock ten o'clock-two o'clock mantra as he matched his actions to the song. He was into his fifth or sixth set when out in the reservoir he saw the side of a good-sized trout as it rolled on the surface. If he adjusted his motion slightly, he thought he could get his fly nearby. He made the cast. 'Okay, not a bad cast; come on fish … bite me.' But as he reeled in without a hit, he knew he would have to try again. Another fish rolled on the surface, then another.

"Hey, Gramps, the fish are breaking the surface but they're not jumping," Brian called loudly to Frank, "what's that all about?"

"I think we might be into a hatching of some sort of insect larvae, but which one I haven't a clue. Some fly fishermen use a small meshed net to get a sample of what's hatching but I don't have one. Keep your eyes open for an insect flying off the water to see what's hatching or we'll have to use trial and error to find one that'll work. You fish that fly for a while and if you don't get a hit, switch to a different nymph, a bugger or a scud. If you get some hits let me know what you're using and I'll do the same for you."

"Okay."

"Okay? Okay? This could be … Grr…ree…aat!" Frank said, imitating Tony the Tiger.

"Sweet."

Six minutes later, with trout continuing to bubble to the surface but without a hit, Brian decided to change flies. He was just putting the finishing touches to the new knot when a small trout rolled about five feet from where he stood. He looked up and noticed an increase in the amount of fish rolling on the surface. He glanced over to his grandfather and realized that Frank was changing flies as well.

"Do you see all these fish? I hope one of these flies is the right one, huh, Gramps?"

Frank answered without looking up, "Yessiree bob! 'cause if we pick a winner we could be in for a great time. The fish are like in a feeding frenzy called the Bite. And it's a whole lot of fun fishin' ... when the Bite is on."

Brian started to work the rod back and forth, ten o'clock-two o'clock, ten o'clock-two o'clock; he liked the rhythm of casting and he hoped he'd picked the right fly. "The Bite huh; well, bite this," he said as he made the cast. He reeled in slowly, expecting a hit at any time. The number of trout in the little cove was unbelievable; fish were rolling everywhere, it seemed. But as Brian finished his retrieve he hadn't had a bite and was thinking he should change flies. 'One more shot with this one, or I'll try something else.' But the second cast just brought more of the same: nothing.

The activity of the fish increased as Brian swiftly changed to a Wooly-Bugger. He liked the name of the fly and the way it looked, like a black fuzzy caterpillar with a hook. 'Maybe this will do the trick,' he hoped. This time when he cast a little farther and started a slow retrieve, he was rewarded with a bump and a few seconds later a hit. "Fish on! Gramps, fish on. One of those Wooly-Buggers, a black one."

"Good going, Boyo; a black Wooly-Bugger it is," Frank answered as he started to reel in faster so he too could change his fly.

Meanwhile, Brian had worked his fish in toward him only to have it get off the hook. One minute he was reeling in a trout and in the next instant, he had an empty line. "Oh, crap," he exclaimed, "he got off."

"Try, try again, m'boy, try, try again."

By this time, not just the water around Brian, but all the water in the cove seemed to be boiling with trout. The rate at which fish broke the surface was amazing. The urgency Brian felt increased;

he couldn't wait to get his line back in the water. He let out line as he worked the rod back and forth. He worked up to a big cast. He looked up to see where he wanted his line to go. Picking a spot a little beyond where his last cast landed, he started to bear down on his rod to snap the line into its final arc. Just then, Brian spotted a large trout that rolled off to the right. He turned his hand slightly in that direction and pushed a little harder to alter where his cast would land. He hoped he might get that big fish to bite.

He snapped his hand forward, pointing the tip of the rod toward the new spot and waited with anticipation. A sharp tug on his right ear was followed by searing pain! His hand dropped the rod and went to his ear. The tug got worse! He found a string or something attached to the pain. Touching it only made it hurt more!

"OW! What the ... Ow!" he yelled. He'd never felt such sharp, intense pain before and was completely taken by surprise. He wanted to escape. He needed to get away! He jumped backwards. This hurt worse! His breaths grew ragged and came faster. Suddenly, he realized what happened; he had hooked himself in the ear and the line, even though it lay limply from his ear, felt like torture. Brian started to shuffle from one foot to the other. This little dance didn't help. He heard himself or dreamed he heard himself screaming over and over, OW ... OW ... OW! He felt foolish but couldn't stop. The thought occurred to him that if he stepped on the rod it might pull his ear off, so he stepped further back. The pain was awful. Finally, he got a firm grasp on the line hanging from his ear and held it up. It still hurt, but only the sharp pain now; he didn't feel the tugging pain. He had a fish hook in his ear!

Abruptly, his grandfather was there. Frank firmly grasped Brian's shoulders and held him. Brian heard his grandfather telling him to stand still. "It's all right, Boyo. It's all right. Stand still Brian. It's all right ... look at me. There ... there. You'll be okay in just a minute. Look at me. Look me in my eyes."

Unfortunate Catch

Brian looked into his grandfather's face and saw the concern written there, but there was also a confidence and a calmness that helped him to settle down. His grandfather reached into the left breast pocket of his fishing vest and came out with a small pair of folding scissors. Frank quickly cut the line to the hook and examined the wounded ear. He said, "Okay, Brian, listen carefully. That hook is right in your ear lobe. It has to come out and it'll hurt. At least it's a barbless hook. Now trust me and don't move. You know what? First, give me your hand."

Brian, puzzled by this request, nevertheless did as he was told and raised his left hand toward his grandfather. Frank firmly held his hand, applying pressure to a spot between his thumb and index finger. At first, this felt uncomfortable, but then Brian realized his ear didn't hurt as much. Then his grandfather reached up with his right hand and firmly held onto the top of Brian's right ear. Pinching there, Frank quickly raised his left hand to pull the hook out. It came out easily with just the slightest tug. Brian reached up and touched his ear. He looked at his fingers. They were bloody. His ear still hurt, but not as much, and suddenly Brian felt really embarrassed. Not only did he manage to hook himself but he'd acted like a big baby.

He couldn't move. His grandfather still held his ear but what held Brian more was Frank's eyes. Concern, love and something else radiated from those eyes. He looked right into Brian and seemed to let him know that it was okay, that his ear would be fine and that he didn't need to feel ashamed of what happened. Brian felt relief wash over him. He could feel himself breathing again; he felt his breath slow. Still he watched his grandfather's face.

After a few moments, Frank held up the black Wooly-Bugger. He shifted his gaze from Brian to the Wooly-Bugger. Frank shook his head in disbelief. He stared at it for an instant. He slightly raised his eyebrows and looked down at the water where trout still rolled at their feet. When he looked up, Frank had a twinkle in his eye and his mouth hinted at a smile and soon they were both laughing.

Thirty minutes later, after Frank had retrieved Brian's fishing rod and stowed all their gear in the boat, he stood on the shore and looked out at the now still water. He waved his hand in the general direction of the cove and said to Brian, who sat on a rock nearby, "You couldn't tell from looking at this cove now there were trout galore just a little while ago, could you? It's quieter than a church on Monday." He glanced at his grandson, who sat quietly holding a small bandage to his ear. Brian looked back and nodded. After cleaning up the wound with a first aid kit, Frank told Brian to sit and rest while he'd gotten things ready for their departure. He thought that they'd better get back as soon as possible so that he could properly care for that ear. He was also a little concerned that Brian might be in shock. At the very least, he knew the boy had had a traumatic experience and would need some time to recover. He sighed with exaggeration and exclaimed, "If only we picked the right fly to match the hatch." He paused before continuing in an Irish brogue, "If ifs and ands were pots and pans, there'd be no trade for tinkers."

Brian smiled, "What? Say that again."

"If ifs and ands were pots and pans there'd be no trade for tinkers. In Ireland, tinkers were like gypsies that traveled around selling and repairing things like pots and pans They also sharpened knives and did odd jobs before moving on to the next town. It's something my grandmother used to say all the time."

On the way back to the campground Frank kept up a constant chatter trying to engage his grandson, but Brian sat silently in the bow and answered direct questions with one-syllable answers, a shrug or a grunt. Frank knew that Brian was coming down from the adrenaline rush that accompanied his panic attack. He noticed Brian shiver despite the warm sunshine, and wanted to get him back to the camper where he could get him some food and change his focus. The hook had left a fairly clean hole and bled freely, but there was still the possibility of infection. He didn't want to take any chances.

He decided then to change their plans and pack everything up and head toward Burns right away. 'The rest of today's fishing is shot. I'll need the big first-aid kit in the camper to clean up Brian's ear, and as long as we have the afternoon to get to Fish Lake, we might as well get an early start.'

Chapter Fifteen

"Hold still, why don't ya … I know it stings, but we gotta get it really well cleaned out. I don't want this getting infected." Frank was bathing Brian's ear with an antiseptic. He rubbed it gently with a soft cloth while Brian squirmed.

"Ow … okay, I'm trying, Owww … that hurts, you know."

"I know, Boyo, I know … I'm almost done for now."

"For now? What did ya mean … for now?"

"Well, I've got good news and bad news. The good news is since it was a barbless hook it left a fairly clean wound. The bad news is we do have to keep it cleaned out. That hook had a lot of bacteria on it, what with it being in a fish's mouth just before you, ahem, caught yourself."

"I thought we agreed not to call it that."

"You agreed not to call it that and you asked me not to, but I do like to use accurate language … especially when it's funny."

"Yeah, right … very funny. You're hilarious."

"It won't be funny if it gets infected. Now, listen. I've been thinking that we ought to get started for Burns right away. I'll get the boat and all the fishing gear packed up. I'd like you to clean up in here," Frank waved his hand about the camper, "and get as much packed and ready as you can. Okay?"

"Sure Gramps, but didn't you want to fish here at Chickahominy some more?"

"Oh, no matter now, the important thing is taking care of that ear. We'll have plenty of time to fish in the Steens."

"But I feel kind of bad, ruining your fishing and all."

"Don't worry about it for a second. Besides," Frank added with a playful smile as he left the camper, "the story alone is better than any fishin'."

Brian laughed, and then called out after his grandfather, "I'm never going to hear the end of this, am I?"

Brian started to pack up the first aid kit, the soap and towels. He found the books and magazines he'd read the night before and remembered his grandfather had taken them out of the cabinet above the table. When he opened the door to put them back he noticed a number of other books. His grandfather had a book on mushrooms and another on birds. There was a book on edible plants and paperbacks of *The Hobbit*, *A Christmas Carol*, *Riders of the Purple Sage*, *Seven Habits of Highly Effective People*, *Foundation*, *East of Eden* and *Man's Search for Meaning*. When Brian placed the fly fishing book back on the shelf he noticed a leather-bound book lying on its side. It looked unusual and had a large, thick rubber band wrapped around it. The front cover was worn but the book gave the appearance of being well cared for. Brian didn't want to be snoopy but felt compelled to open it just to see what it was. Opening it, he found the title in bold black writing: MY BULLETIN BOARD. Brian thumbed through it quickly and noticed his grandfather had made notes on books he had read, movies he had seen and had collected a number of quotes that lay scattered throughout. In the back were folded pages that included newspaper and magazine articles as well as other writings. 'I've got to ask him about this,' he thought, as he replaced the rubber band before returning the book to its resting place.

Soon, the camper was almost ready to go. Brian stepped outside to see if he could help his grandfather. The bright sunlight made him squint and he noticed how hot it had become. A dry wind from the west gusted just as he stepped down off the camper and blew dust past his feet. He wondered if it would get as windy today as it was yesterday when they pulled in. He wouldn't miss that.

"Hey Gramps, need a hand with anything?" he called over to Frank, who was busy with the boat.

"Yeah, great ... thanks, Boyo, come get this gear and put it on the table. We're just about ready to pack it all up and get on our way. This time, I'm going to hitch up the trailer and back it on down to get the boat. That way, I can leave some of the gear in the boat. It'll save some on trips and time."

Frank carried the rods and the cooler back up to the camper and soon had the camper packed and the trailer hitched to the truck. He carefully backed the trailer down the boat ramp until most of it was under water. He walked to the back of the truck and climbed onto the tongue of the trailer. Brian watched as Frank fiddled with the small hand-powered winch until the nylon rope, which sported a hook at the end, fed freely. He pulled out a good length of the rope and then turned to Brian. "Here, catch this and attach it to that bracket ... right there at the bow of the boat. Okay, Brian?"

"Yeah, sure, Gramps; no problem."

When that was done, Brian untied the ropes holding the boat to the pier allowing Frank to ratchet the boat up onto the trailer using the winch. When it was completely up and secured, Frank drove slowly up the boat ramp. The trailer and boat dripped water all the way to their campsite. After packing up the rest of the gear into the camper and into the boat, Frank, with Brian's help, placed the tarp once more over the boat and secured everything with some tie-downs and bungee cords. He looked over his handiwork and nodded, "Looks like we're just about to hit the road, Brian. Let's police the campsite and make sure we don't leave any trash lying around. Okay?"

They both walked about, picking up a bottle cap here and piece of plastic there, but their campsite was fairly clean. Frank looked at the campsite next to theirs, where the old man and his wife had been. "They must have pulled out while we were fishing," he said. There was a small collection of trash scattered about and Frank walked over to clean up this mess as well. He explained to Brian that he always liked to leave a place better than the way he found it. "Besides," he added, "I'd hate to have a nice family come into this campsite and find trash on the ground. It only takes a minute, and if everyone felt the same way it would make for a better world, don't you think?"

"I guess, but they should have cleaned up their own mess."

"That may be, but since they didn't, I have a chance to be of service," Frank said with a nod of his head as he proceeded to clean up the area.

"Okay Boyo … looks good. I guess we can get started. I'll drive on into Burns. Later, you can drive us to Frenchglen and I'll drive into the campground at Fish Lake. Oh! And … we might as well have an early dinner in Burns. It'll save us some time." Frank climbed into the truck and smiled over at his grandson, "Well Brian, say goodbye to Chickahominy Reservoir, where you caught your first big trout."

"Yeah, and where I got a hook in my ear too."

The tires whined as the dry, windswept desert of Eastern Oregon sped by. Brian, slumped in the passenger seat, settled into an uneasy silence. Frank wondered what he was feeling and wanted to keep him amused until they got to town. He reached over to lower the volume on the music. "Brian, have I ever told you any of my nun stories?"

Brian glanced up puzzled, "Nun stories?"

"Well, yeah … you know I went to Catholic school. And most of the teachers in my grammar school were nuns. Now, these women may have joined the order out of a sincere desire to serve, but I think something must have gone wrong with their perspective or attitude, 'cause some of those nuns were not nice people. I remember being taught about one of the Gospels where Jesus was quoted as saying "suffer the little children," which I interpret as meaning to be patient with them. Well, the nuns must have interpreted that differently because they seemed to have a wide variety of ways to make us suffer."

Frank spoke in a light, entertaining manner and the way he told this story led Brian to believe that it was one of his favorites. He also knew his grandfather well enough to realize that he was just warming up. The bright smile, the warm words spoken with just a touch of irony, and Frank's storytelling skills combined to kindle a clear sense of anticipation. Brian turned in his seat and smiled back at his grandfather.

Frank continued, "Suffer ... they could make school a living hell. Now Brian, you have to understand that times were different back then. Some of the stuff that was accepted then would not be tolerated nowadays. Heck, I remember my mother telling one of my teachers that if I misbehaved and she needed to let me have it ... then by all means, Sister, let him have it. She was giving this nun permission to hit me. Moreover, we were taught to just stand there and take it. Now, I was no angel and I knew I would get in trouble sooner or later and here I was standing next to my mother while she was giving this nun free rein. I remember thinking, oh no Mom, what are you saying? Some nuns didn't need any encouragement at all to hit us kids."

"I remember my first day of school ... my first day! My mother walks me to school and with all the kids lining up in front of the school ... she points over to the other kindergarten kids and tells me, now Frankie, there are your friends. See, there's Kevin and Jimmy and Bobby, so you just go on over there and the nun will take care of you. But she didn't let me go right over. Oh, no ... she grabs me in her arms and starts giving me this hug. My baby, she says, you're getting so big, and today's your first day of school; then she starts crying. Okay, so now I'm wrapped up in my mother's arms while she's crying and all I want to do is go to school and besides, I didn't want the other kids to see my mother hugging me, but I couldn't move. I'm totally enveloped in this vice-like hug by a woman who's chosen this moment to have some sort of maternal meltdown. Finally, she lets me go and boy oh boy, did I go."

"Now here I am ... a kindergartener, what, six years old ... excited to be finally going to school but just a minute late getting into line. So, I went to the back of the line, not realizing that all the rest of kids were lined up in size order, with the smallest kids in front, to the biggest kids in back. I was a small kid, in fact, I was usually near the front of the line throughout the rest of my years there; anyway, my friend Kevin O'Hara was the tallest kid in the class, so I just walked up to him and said 'Hi.' The school had a marching band, in fact, my aunts had been members. The band was playing something I didn't recognize, and the music, combined with my enthusiasm, soon had my feet moving ... it was like I couldn't stand still; I was that excited. Then, all of a sudden, I felt myself lifted off my feet by my ear! Some nun is slapping me and screaming at me how dare you dance during the 'Star Spangled Banner!' And why aren't you in your proper place in line? And the whole time she's yelling at me she's slapping me and yanking on my ear. So here I am crying and trying to stand as tall as I could 'cause she was really hurting my ear."

"But she doesn't stop. Instead, she drags me over to the principal and tells her, Sister, this young man, I was six for God's sake, this young man, was dancing during the 'Star Spangled Banner' and wasn't in his proper place in line! So the principal gives me a look that would have curdled milk and reaches out and grabs my hair right here," Frank held the top of his sideburn, "she yanked on it and slapped my face in time to her yells, you will not dance ... during the 'Star Spangled Banner' ... and you will find your proper place ... in line. When she finally let me go, the first nun, Sister Mary Rogers, whom we kids later called 'Jolly Roger' — you know, like the skull and crossbones, the pirate flag — she brings me back to the line and thrusts me toward another nun saying, I believe this one is yours sister; he was dancing during the 'Star Spangled Banner!' Now, by this time I imagined every nun in the place taking turns with me and I flinched as this new one reached toward me, but instead of more abuse, she brushed my hair with her hand and said to the other nun, thank you Sister, and to me she says, let's get you into line, at which the first nun says oh, and he wasn't in size order either, to which the new nun says again, but this time colder, thank you Sister. That second nun was Sister Priscilla, one of the nicest teachers I ever had—well I guess kindergarten teachers are supposed to be nice —but she sure was a good teacher and one of the nicest nuns I ever met."

Frank paused as much to laugh at his own story as to catch his breath. Brian sat doubled over in laughter. The story itself was terrible but Frank told it so well and with such humor Brian couldn't help but laugh. "That's horrible, Gramps ... what a first day of school. I'll bet you behaved yourself after that, huh?"

"Well, I always lined up correctly after that and you better believe I stood still during the 'Star Spangled Banner,' but I wouldn't exactly say I behaved myself. I was always one of those kids, you know the type ... that felt like all the rules didn't necessarily apply to them. Anyway, during my nine years at good old Saint Camillus I had my share of run-ins with the nuns. I swear, some of those nuns were real witches, or ahem, rhymes with witches." Then Frank smiled and added, "Of course, I did get even."

"You got even?"

"Yep. I got even. Do ya want to hear about it?"

"You bet."

"Okay. First, I have to explain about two of our teachers; Sister Frances Denise and Sister Mary Herbert. First, Sister Frances Denise, better known as Frannie or The Penguin."

"The Penguin?" Brian interrupted.

"Yeah, The Penguin. All the nuns looked more or less like penguins 'cause the habits, ah, uniforms were black robes with a white board over their chests and a white deal that covered their foreheads. See, black and white like a penguin. But Frannie ... she didn't just look like a penguin, she actually waddled like one too. She was our seventh-grade teacher. One day, for some reason, she was taking our class downstairs. The upstairs classrooms were reached by a long hallway that ran the length of the building with staircases at each end of the hall. The back staircase was rarely used. Well anyway, here we are lined up in size order, boys on one side of the hallway, girls on the other and she walks, or should I say waddles, to the head of the line and says, follow me class."

Frank looked over to Brian to see if his grandson was following along and continued when Brian nodded. "So she says, follow me class. So, off we go. She was leading us toward the front of the building. Anyway, we start following her down the hallway and without a word, one of the guys up near the front of the line starts to waddle just like Frannie; I mean just like her ... in perfect time ... in step, left-right-left-right. Before long, the entire line of boys was waddling in step, and in time, right behind The Penguin. When she moved left, we moved left; when she moved right, we moved right. We were all laughing silently and havin' a great time right up until the moment we heard the principal's voice yell out, Sister Frances Denise! Stop your class right now!"

"The principal had come up the little-used back stairway just in time to see the march of the penguins. Every boy knew we were in trouble. She walked up and whispered something into Frannie's ear and turned to the class. She looked up the line of boys; she looked down the line of boys. If any one of us would have smiled or laughed we would have all been dead and we knew it. There was not the slightest movement from any of us. Finally the principal said, all the boys in this class will report to me when school is over. I will be calling each of your parents to let them know why you will be late getting home today. That is all."

"Did you get in a lot of trouble, Gramps?"

"Not really; as I recall we had to clean up some junk in one of the old buildings on the school grounds. We even had fun doing it. And, as far as my parents were concerned, well, my old man thought it was funny and my mom tried to act shocked, but I think she thought it was funny too."

"But you were saying you got even?"

"That's right, where was I? Oh yeah, Frannie. She really wasn't as bad as some of the others; if Frannie hit you it was generally for a good reason. Funny thing about her, I used to read other books during class, pretty much whatever I had at the time; mysteries, Sherlock Holmes, sports stories … whatever, and during the day, if Frannie called on me and I was reading, she would make me bring her the book. Then I would go back to my desk and after a while start reading another book. She'd catch me again and make me turn it over as well. Sometimes she would end up with three or four of my books. She never gave me too hard a time over this and would give 'em all back at the end of the day. There were times when I was reading four or five books at the same time and other times when she would confiscate and return the same book day after day until I finished it. So, really, she wasn't too bad, but one day I'm sitting at my desk, minding my own business, mind you, when she calls on me. Frank, says she, did you do your homework? To which I replied, yes Sister. And did you read the section in the catechism? Yes Sister. Now, this whole time I was racking my brain trying to remember what it was we had for homework and what in the catechism assignment might be important. So then, she says, why don't you tell the class what Jesus said on the banks of the Jordan?"

"I didn't know. What did Jesus say on the banks of the Jordan? I had no idea. So there I am trying to remember what Jesus said on the banks of the Jordan and for the life of me I couldn't come up with an answer ... nothing ... not even a lame attempt at something. I paused and said, Sister, I don't know. Now, there was something about my answer or the way I said it that really set her off, 'cause the next thing I know, she comes charging down the aisle, pulls me out of my seat and proceeds to really let me have it. I mean the whole works; hair-pulling, shaking, slapping." Frank continued with a chuckle, "I think I was lucky she didn't have a baseball bat handy."

"Anyway, when she got tired of hitting me, she walked back up to the front of the class and called on someone else. But the question of whatever the hell Jesus said on the banks of the Jordan never did get answered. So I opened up the book and thumbed through to that section. I read it once. I read it again. I got mad. I became overwhelmed with righteous indignation. I became furious. My arm shot up like that of the little brownnose kid from the front of the class who knows the answer to something and can't wait to show off, and it stayed up. Frannie glanced at me and looked away. The other kids near me whispered put your arm down, are you crazy? Put your arm down ... but my arm stayed up. Finally, she looks at me and says through clenched teeth, yes Frank, and I say, Sister I'd like to read something from the catechism ... she says, again, through clenched teeth, go ahead Frank. So, this is what I read ... and Jesus stood on the banks of the Jordan and looked up to heaven AS IF TO SAY—"

Frank looked over at Brian, who nodded, before continuing, "I repeated, as IF to say. Then I said, Sister, why don't YOU tell the class what Jesus said on the banks of the Jordan?"

"Her answer came as quick as a bolt of lightning ... she charged down the aisle and let me have it again, but at least I had the satisfaction of being right. Well, I learned two valuable lessons that day," Frank's laughter spiced his words, "never give in to righteous indignation ... at least not on the spur of the moment and ... never show up another person, especially someone with power."

"Okay, so what's this about getting even?"

"I'm gettin' there; be patient. Okay, so that's Frannie, then there was Herbie, or should I say, Sister Mary Herbert. She was a witch. Herbie was our eighth-grade teacher and she really had it in for me. I suffered through a number of pretty good slappings throughout the year but a month or so before we were to graduate she really got me. At one point in what was already a good face-slapping she reached up and grabbed my ears and shook my head back and forth. Her fingernails were long and probably not all that clean; they cut me ... right here behind my ear." Frank pointed to the back of his ear; he continued, "The blood ran down my neck and stained my collar ... I still have scars back there from it. Well, anyway, I get home and my mom sees the stains so I tell her what happened. She cleans it up and says Frankie, come with me. We're going to the convent to see Sister Mary Herbert. The last thing I wanted to do was go see Sister Mary Herbert. I begged her not to ... I implored her not to ... to no avail, my mom had her mind made up, so off we go to the convent, which was next to the school. First, my mother speaks with the principal and a little while later Herbie comes to the door. My mom says to her, I saw what you did to my son's ears and I want you to know that if you do anything else to him for the rest of this year, I will personally come down here and beat the shit out of you, lady. You got that? Mom didn't call her Sister ... she said 'lady.' Later, on the way home, my mom told me to defend myself from Herbie if she tried that again."

"Wow! So, how did you get even?"

"I'm gettin' there. I'm gettin' there. Well, I had no more problems with Herbie after that. I soon graduated and went on to high school. But, about three years later, I was driving along Rockaway Beach Boulevard after a heavy summer rainstorm when who do I see walking on the sidewalk two blocks away but Herbie, Frannie and some poor innocent bystander nun. The storm drains had filled and there was a big puddle next to them. Well, I hit that puddle doing about 40 miles an hour and I hit it fat. When I turned my head to see, I caught a glimpse of a wall of water hovering above the three nuns ... with them looking up at it. I drove four or five blocks and laughed so hard I had to pull over."

"Did they know it was you?"

"Nope."

Chapter Sixteen

"Hey Gramps, we just passed a sign; we're coming up on Burns in five miles."

"Yep. I saw it too. Keep your eyes open for a likely place for us to eat and a gas station; we need to top off the gas."

Before long, Frank spotted a gas station on the left. He slowed down, pulled into the center turn lane and when traffic permitted, drove into the gas station. He stopped at an empty pump and waited for an attendant to come over. To Brian he explained, "In Oregon you can't pump your own gas. There's no self-serve allowed."

The attendant, a tall thin young man who looked to be about 19 or 20 years old, approached the truck and asked with a smile, "What can I do for you?"

"Fill 'er up, regular, please."

"You got it."

While the attendant was busy doing that, Frank turned to Brian and said, "We could stop at a supermarket and get a few things. Do you want to eat something while we drive or would you rather stop somewhere?"

"Whatever."

"Now, what's that supposed to mean?"

"It means whatever; I don't care one way or the other. What do you want to do?"

"I don't know. We've got plenty of time to get into camp. I suppose we might as well stop in for a meal."

"Okay."

"Okay. Great, then what kinda food would you like?"

"Whatever."

"Again with the 'whatever' ... how about some canned dog food?"

"Yuck."

"So, it's not really whatever. You might actually have a preference. Well, let's think about it then. We're smack-dab in the middle of cattle country and so we might try a steak place; or would you prefer seafood?"

The attendant interrupted with the receipt. Frank took it from him with a thank you, started the truck and carefully pulled out of the gas station. He turn to Brian and looked about to say something when Brian said, "Steak. Steak sounds good."

Frank smiled and replied, "Okay, steak it is."

They hadn't traveled more than 10 minutes before Brian noted a small restaurant that boasted homemade pies. "How 'bout there, Gramps?" he asked.

"Okay with me."

The parking lot had ample room for the truck and the trailer so Frank pulled into two spots, turned the truck off and stated matter-of-factly, "The parking lot is not that full. Of course, it's only three-fifteen; it's still a little early for dinner yet."

Brian slid out of the passenger seat, closed his door and walked around the front of the truck toward his grandfather.

Frank waited for Brian before heading toward the restaurant. He said as if to no one in particular, "Whenever I visit a new restaurant I like to pick one that seems real busy. The locals usually know where the best food in town is. But, like I said, it is early."

When they reached the entrance, Brian reached out to open the door for Frank.

Frank said, "Thank you, Brian." As they entered the restaurant Frank noticed a counter on the left, lined with stools. A wall with a pass-through window separated the area behind the counter from the kitchen. Next to the counter stood an upright display case whose rotating shelves held a few whole pies as well as some individual slices of assorted pie. There were fruit pies and cream pies as well as two slices of what looked to be coconut custard. They looked appealing. Frank finished examining the pies, then turned to Brian with a smile and a wink, commenting, "A nice piece o' pie is a thing of beauty."

The dining area contained about 10 tables with some booths along the walls. He noticed a small hallway on his immediate left that held the restrooms. Frank turned to Brian and said, "I'm going to use the facilities. Why don't you grab a booth and I'll be right out."

"Sure thing, Gramps."

The wooden restroom door had a brass handle and as Frank reached for it he made a note that the wood was slightly discolored in and around the handle and could have used a wipe. The bathroom itself was fairly clean, although the wastebasket was full. When Frank turned the water on to wash his hands he jumped back slightly because the water spit out of the faucet, threatening to splash his pants. He shook his head as he dried his hands before joining Brian.

His grandson sat in a booth directly across from the counter. Frank slid into the booth. Brian welcomed his grandfather with a curt nod and a wave of his hand.

"There's no blueberry. I always get blueberry pie, with a scoop of vanilla ice cream; always ... and they're out."

"Life does have its disappointments now and again, now doesn't it? What exactly do you mean by always?"

"I've tried some other kinds of pie before, and I always come back to blueberry. I like blueberry."

"You really mean always?"

"Yes." Brian somehow felt as if he should defend himself. "I really like blueberry."

"I'm sure you do Boyo; I'm sure you do. But, how can you be so sure? Without trying something new once in a while, don't you run the risk of getting stale, of getting into a rut?"

Dinner Stop

"It's just pie."

"There is one of those four letter words I really dislike: 'just'. It's right up there with can't. How many things in life are just this, or just that, escaping our attention, or worse, are not deemed worthy of our best effort. I'm talking now about paying attention to the little things and making an effort to do one's best. You know … if a thing's worth doing, it's worth doing right."

"Whatever."

"Does 'whatever' mean be quiet too?"

Brian looked up at his grandfather and laughed. "Sometimes."

"There's another word I'm beginning to dislike. It's not precise. It has a variety of meanings that can lead to misunderstandings. I'd prefer that you simply tell me to be quiet."

"Aw, Gramps, it's not like that. I just don't feel like a lecture right now. I'm hungry and thirsty."

"Okay, Brian. That's fine," Frank said with a smile. "Please just tell me whenever I'm talking too much and I'll try to curb my tongue."

The discussion ended when the waitress, a small, middle-aged woman with her light brown hair tied up in a bun, walked up to their table carrying two menus and two glasses of water. She greeted them hurriedly and placed the glasses, ice clinking, on the table. "Here are your menus; the special today is a T-bone steak, with your choice of mashed, baked, or French fried potatoes, sautéed veggies, a homemade biscuit or Texas toast and your choice of soup or salad. The soups today are chicken noodle or navy bean."

While Brian quickly downed his water, Frank looked up at the waitress and asked, "And how much is the special?"

"Oh, it's fourteen ninety-five." She watched as Brian set down his glass and added, "Looks like you're thirsty; I'll bring you some more water right away."

Brian smiled and said, "I am, thank you."

"Well, take your time. Look at your menus and I'll be right back with your water." With that, she turned and walked purposely toward the kitchen.

Frank looked over to Brian and asked, "Does that T-bone sound good to you?"

"It sure does."

"What's your impression, so far, of this place?"

"Okay, I guess. The waitress seemed kind of preoccupied or something."

"Very good, Brian; she did, didn't she? And did you catch her name?"

"No, but she's coming right back with more water."

"Here you are, gentlemen. As quickly as you drank that down you must be thirsty, so I'm just going to leave this here," she said, indicating the pitcher as she placed it on the table after refilling Brian's glass and topping off Frank's. "I'll be back shortly to answer any questions you might have."

Again, she quickly strode to the kitchen, leaving Frank and Brian sharing the same surprised expression on their faces.

Brian shook his head and drank another glass of water. Frank sipped his, wondering if they had made a good decision coming into this place.

Before too long the waitress returned. She pulled a small order booklet out of her apron with one hand and a pen in the other. She clicked the pen, held it hovering above the pad and looked at Frank expectantly.

"I'll have the special, please, with the biscuit."

"Great! How do you like your steak, sir?" she asked in a happy and cheerful manner.

"Medium rare, please."

"Soup or salad?"

"Soup ... the chicken noodle."

"Great! And you, young man?"

"I'll have the same except with salad."

"Medium rare good for you too?"

"Yes, please."

"Okay. For dressings we have honey mustard, ranch, raspberry vinaigrette, and our house special is creamy garlic."

"Ranch, please."

"Anything besides water for either of you gentlemen?"

Brian spoke right up, "Sure, can I have an iced tea?"

"Okay, one iced tea." Turning back to Frank she added, "And for you, sir?"

"Water is fine for now. I'll have some coffee, later, maybe with some pie." Frank stressed the word pie and smiled at Brian with a kind of goofy, questioning look.

Brian laughed and said, "I guess I'll have some pie too, but," he added to the waitress, "you're all out of my favorite."

"And what is your favorite?"

"Blueberry."

"Blueberry, huh, well I've got some good news for you. We're a little shorthanded right now, so the fresh pies haven't made it out to the display case yet," she nodded her head knowingly. "But I happen to know there are some blueberry pies, made with fresh Oregon blueberries, still cooling off in the kitchen. They're warm, and if you like your pie á la mode you are in for a treat."

"I do; that's exactly how I like it."

"Well then, that's how you'll get it. Let me get your order started. Let me know if there's anything else you want. I'll be right back with your soup," she said to Frank, "and your salad, young man." The waitress quickly did an about-face and marched off toward the counter. Frank watched as she attached their order to a clip on an old ticket wheel suspended above the counter, rang the bell and announced in a loud voice, "Order up. I need a chicken soup and a salad." She then said in a softer voice, "Bert, I need someone to bus some tables." The waitress quickly visited some of the other diners, sporting a coffee pot in each hand.

Frank chuckled at Brian, "Okay, so you're gonna get your blueberry pie after all, and she made it sound so good I think I'll join you."

"Yeah man," Brian rubbed his hands together, smiled at his grandfather and added, "warm blueberry pie ... yummyyyy."

"Now this is more like it, Brian."

The waitress returned to the counter, both coffee pots empty. She quickly started a new pot to brewing, grabbed a wash cloth from a bucket under the counter and proceeded to wipe the counter. She looked up toward the kitchen and said in a firm voice, "I still need those tables bused, Bert; can you please send Thomas out here?"

From the kitchen a voice answered, "Just a minute Diane, he'll be right out."

The sound of clinking dishes filtered into the dining area and Frank could hear muffled voices in conversation. A few minutes later a thin, gangly young man emerged with a large plastic container and started to clear the dirty dishes from a table on the far side of the dining room. His apron was a little wet and he was obviously sweating and hot. To Frank he seemed to be careful as he placed the dishes into the container, but his speed did not match the urgent pace shown by the waitress. In the meantime, the waitress picked up their soup and salad from the shelf and brought them right over to their table. "Here's your soup, sir," she said as she placed it in front of Frank and the salad in front of Brian, adding, "and your salad. Is there anything else I can get you gentlemen right now?"

Frank looked down at his soup and said, "As a matter fact, there is. Could you bring me my biscuit now, please? I'd like it with the soup."

"Certainly. I'll be right back." Again she strode quickly toward the kitchen and said over the counter to the cook, "Bert, I need a biscuit for table two now. When is Meg coming in?"

The response from the kitchen was an emphatic, "Soon, I hope. Here's your biscuit."

"Thanks."

As the waitress returned with Frank's biscuit the phone rang. She placed the plate quickly in front of him and hustled over to the register to answer it. Frank pulled open the biscuit and started buttering it. He heard the waitress say, "His temperature is what? You're sure? You gave him some Tylenol an hour ago. Okay, I'll be right home; we need to get him into urgent care. Yes, I'll be there in just a few minutes. Get him ready to go."

Frank watched as she removed her apron and set it down beside the register. She walked over toward the kitchen and spoke quietly to someone behind the counter and then without delay she hurried from the restaurant.

Frank turned to Brian and said, "If they were shorthanded before now they're really in a bind. We just lost our waitress."

Brian placed a forkful of salad in his mouth. Chewing slowly, he turned to watch the waitress leave the building and walk toward a small sedan. As she opened the door, Brian swallowed and replied, "This can't be good."

"It might be okay. Our order has already been placed. With any luck we'll get our food and be on our way."

"But," Brian seemed suddenly worried, "what about our pie? I was really looking forward to that pie. Today has been terrible so far." Brian seemed crestfallen. "I hooked myself fishin', so we had to leave early and, well, I wanted some pie, that's all."

"So, you think today has been terrible, huh?"

"Yes!"

"Let me tell you a story that I heard a long time ago that has always helped me put things in perspective. Tony told this to me once, I think, when I was complaining about having a bad day. It seemed his mother's older brother was in the Italian army during World War I. He was stationed along the Bulgarian border where there was some horrendous fighting; trench warfare; bitter, bitter fighting. It was really bad. Well, anyway, this uncle, if I remember correctly, was named Dominic, he got shot in the face. The bullet entered his mouth and blew away part of his face. He lost all the teeth on one side of his mouth and the bullet broke his jaw. Obviously, he was knocked out." Frank paused for a moment, took a spoonful of soup, then continued, "When he regained consciousness he heard voices nearby and realized they were enemy soldiers who must have captured the Italian trenches. He knew that if they thought he was still alive they would stick a bayonet in him so he lay still until sometime later when he again lost consciousness."

Frank took a sip of water before continuing, "He woke up during the night. The stars above shown brightly and for the moment there was quiet. He didn't know if the Bulgarians were still there and he felt too weak to move anyway. So he just lay there looking up at the stars. He said later that he never saw more beautiful stars in his life and, for the rest of his life, never looked up at the night sky without experiencing a tremendous feeling of gratitude. Well, anyway, he drifted back off again and when he came to, he found himself unable to move or see anything. He had been thrown on a pile of dead bodies with more added on top of him. When the Italians recaptured the trenches later, his countrymen found him and realized he was still alive. They sent him to the hospital where he eventually recovered. It had been three days."

"Wow!" Brian said. "That's incredible."

"That's not all."

Dinner Stop

"There's more?"

"Much more ... when Dominic recovered, even though his face was terribly disfigured, he was sent back to the front. Today, of course, he would have been sent home, but in those days they just got him well and sent him back to fight. Later in the war he was serving under a captain that had lost both of his brothers along the same stretch of trenches they were still fighting over. A successful attack had captured some enemy soldiers who had surrendered. But instead of sending these prisoners back to the Italian POW area, as was normal procedure, he had them held in a nearby grotto, under guard. The captain knew about the ordeal Dominic had survived and his disfigured face so he selected Dominic to execute this group of prisoners. He had a machine gun set up and ordered Tony's uncle to shoot them. He refused. The captain threatened to shoot Dominic himself if he did not obey his order. He still refused. The captain ordered some other Italian soldiers to put Dominic with the Bulgarian soldiers and to machine-gun them all down. They refused too. Eventually, the captain was restrained and a superior officer called for. The captain was relieved of command and the prisoners taken to the POW camp. The Red Cross was in the area at the time and somehow got wind of this incident. The Italian Army made a big thing about it and gave Dominic a medal for refusing to obey the order to kill the prisoners. Tony told me his uncle would often laugh about being the only soldier in the Italian army that ever got a medal for not following orders."

Frank placed a spoonful of soup in his mouth followed by a piece of biscuit and chewed thoughtfully before he continued, "You know, Brian, if his wound had not looked so bad to those enemy soldiers, if even once one of them had checked to see if he was still alive, he would have been killed. Can you picture it? Scared soldiers, stuck in an Italian trench, with the threat of violent death ever present; the stench of death filling the air, the bodies of dead soldiers from both sides lying in the bottom of the trench and there's an Italian soldier with half his face shot off. They must have looked away whenever they looked at him or one of them would have noticed him breathing. The horrible nature of his wound saved his life."

"That's amazing!"

"Yes it is. And, the rest of the story is truly an inspiration. Dominic returned to the small Italian village he was from. He never felt sorry for himself even though he had been left so disfigured. Eventually, he married and raised a family and became known as the happiest man in the town. He always felt gratitude for his life and appreciated every extra day of living. When he died the entire town mourned. Tony told me that his mother would often talk about her brother and the story she liked to tell the most was about how Dominic would walk at night just to look up at the stars to remember, and wonder."

Chapter Seventeen

Brian quietly picked at his salad. His grandfather had just finished another story that left him thinking. In almost any situation, Frank seemed able to tell a story to help Brian see things in a different light. 'Today sure has had its moments,' he thought, 'but it wasn't all that bad.' His ear really hurt when he hooked it, but felt much better now. Brian thought back to when his parents first talked to him about this camping trip. He remembered complaining about having to spend a week alone with his grandfather, and wondering what he would do to pass the time. His dad told him it would be fine. Here was a chance to get to know your grandfather better, he'd said, and there ain't nothing wrong with a little fishin' and campin'. When his electronics were stolen, Brian really thought he would be bored, but they'd been so busy that he'd been anything but. This camping trip had become transformed into something beyond just a chance for him to share some time with his grandfather; it had taken on a feeling of adventure.

"Hey Gramps, today after I hooked myself you pressed my hand right here." Brian held out his hand, pointing to the spot, before continuing, "You also pinched my ear before you removed the hook. What's that all about? What did that do?"

"Well Brian, the human body truly is a miracle. There are lots of nerve endings throughout the body; some of them have pressure points that when pressed or massaged can help relieve pain or discomfort. Years ago I spent some time learning about this stuff. I studied, you know, books on acupressure, massage, and other related fields, like shiatsu therapy. I have a list of books in my journal on the subject if you'd like to study up on it yourself or I could show you a couple of simple ones."

"That would be cool. Oh! That reminds me; I looked at a book called 'My Bulletin Board', what's that?"

"It's kind of a journal."

"Why call a journal your bulletin board?"

"It's not a conventional journal. It's not like a diary; it's more like a collection of things, quotes I like or books on certain subjects, newspaper articles or other stuff I found to be of interest … kind of like a bulletin board."

"Oh, I see. Would you mind if I looked through it?"

"Not at all. Be my guest."

Brian nodded in agreement and replied, "Sweet."

Frank tilted his bowl to one side and scooped up the last spoonful of soup. As he finished his soup he noticed the boy, Thomas, walk quickly from the kitchen to the men's room. Frank wondered out loud, "Without a waitress it'll be interesting to see how soon our steaks get here."

Brian looked around and replied, "And our pie."

Frank watched an older couple, finished with their meal, get up from their table and wait for a minute at the register. Not seeing anyone available to take their money the gentleman tapped a small bell near the register to get some help. After 30 seconds or so he rang the bell again, this time with a bit more impatience. The cook emerged from the kitchen looking somewhat stressed. He apologized to the customers for their wait and rang up the sale. As they left, he stole a glance around the restaurant before returning to the kitchen.

"That poor guy looks more than a little stressed out. And it is almost dinner time." Frank paused a moment before asking, "I wonder how busy they are for dinner?"

Brian just shrugged as he finished his salad.

Drumming his fingers on the table, Frank thought back to the Appetitto Shop and how busy they'd been at times. 'On a hot summer day, the crowds coming to the beach would start trickling in about mid-morning. As the day wore on and the temperature rose, customers formed a steady stream throughout lunch and beyond. The limited space behind the counter would require all of us to work together to handle those extended rushes. Then, there was that one day when Charlie got sick; he still tried to work but Tony sent him home. That day was really nuts. The customers kept coming, nobody had time for a break, and without Charlie an important part of the team was missing. Tony worried we weren't waiting on customers fast enough and said so more than once.' Frank smiled when he recalled that right after lunch Tony's son just happened to stop in to get cold cuts for his family. When Sonny saw the situation, he quickly got behind the counter and pitched in. 'Somehow, with his help, we managed to get through the rest of the day.'

Frank's daydream was suddenly cut short when he noticed the cook place two plates under a heat lamp on the shelf of the pass-through window. The cook tapped a small bell twice. Frank realized that Thomas was still in the bathroom and wondered how long their dinners were going to sit under the heat lamp. He felt tempted to go get them himself but thought that might embarrass his grandson. He decided to be patient and see what happened. Just as he thought that they'd waited long enough and was getting ready to get the dinners himself, he heard the toilet flush. Shortly, Thomas emerged from the bathroom and walked toward the kitchen. Frank watched him carefully. When the boy started to walk by the shelf that held the food he noticed the two dinners. Thomas seemed to hesitate a moment before picking them up. He started toward Frank and Brian.

Frank shook his head no, looked Thomas right in the eyes and said, "Stop right there! I know you didn't wash your hands after using the bathroom. We will not accept this food and I would like to speak to the manager."

The boy turned a bright red, started to make a response but only managed a very quiet, "I'm s...s...sorry." He walked slowly toward the kitchen, placed the dinners on the counter and disappeared into the kitchen. Frank heard him say, "Bert, I'm sorry, I ... the guy at table two wants to see you."

"You mean the customer, right?"

"Yeah, the customer."

Frank gave Brian a reassuring look in answer to Brian's puzzled expression. He watched as the cook slowly emerged from the kitchen, pausing only to look at the two dinners still sitting on the counter. 'So the cook is the owner. He looks beat.' As Bert started toward them, Frank stood up and with a smile, raised his hands, palms outward, to show Bert a calm attitude. He said, "The boy didn't wash his hands before bringing us our food."

Bert stammered a response, "I'm terribly sorry ... you have my sincerest apology. He's new and the regular cook is on vacation, we're really shorthanded, the dishwasher is broke and we're having to hand-wash everything." He stopped, wiped his hand across his forehead then abruptly added, "There's no excuse. What can we do the make this up to you?"

Frank thought carefully about his reply. He was about to speak when the door of the restaurant opened and a middle-aged woman purposely walked in wearing the uniform of a waitress. She seemed to quickly size up the situation and said, "Is there a problem, Bert? What can I do to help?"

"Oh, Meg, thank goodness, Thomas brought them their dinners without washing his hands after using the bathroom. I was just asking this gentleman what we needed to do."

"Okay ... go on back to the kitchen and I'll take care of them."

"Thanks Meg." Bert replied with obvious relief, and to Frank added, "Meg'll take good care of you. If you want, I'll re-fire those steaks right away. We'll get you your dinners ASAP."

Frank looked from Bert to Meg. He didn't know what to say.

Meg nodded her head knowingly, "You probably have been waiting for your food for a while already and you're not sure you want to wait any more, right?"

"Well, yes and no."

"They ordered the specials." Bert added, "I can have two new dinners right out, sir, if that would be okay with you."

"Sir, Bert does a great job on those steaks and dessert is on us. Okay?"

"Well, I suppose that works." Frank replied as he sat back down.

Meg beamed a big smile, turned to Bert and said, "Okay! Let's get a move on. We have customers to impress."

Bert turned toward the kitchen and hurried away. Meg spoke to Frank, "Thank you. You won't regret it. Let me get settled in and I'll be right back to check on you."

"We're okay for now; we just want our dinners."

"They will be ready shortly. I'll bring them as soon as they're ready and thanks again."

Meg strode into the kitchen and Frank heard her say, "There's no need to fear, mighty Meg is here."

Frank explained to Brian, "I hate to make a fuss in a restaurant but some things are just not acceptable."

"Good thing we're not in a hurry, huh, gramps?"

"That's right, but I think this waitress, Meg, is impressive. Without her confidence and her reassurance that everything would be okay, I'm not sure we would be staying. There's something about her I like."

"She is kind of cute, for an older woman, that is."

Frank laughed, "She doesn't look nearly as old as I am."

"Nobody looks that old."

"Funny ... very funny."

The two travelers sat waiting for their steaks in silence. Frank, lost in thought, drummed his fingers while Brian pulled out a brochure on the Steens Mountain he'd found in the truck. As Brian read about the Steens, Frank noticed Meg make her way around the other tables, checking on the diners still eating, delivering food, taking an order for dessert and clearing the empty tables as she went. 'She's a pretty woman,' Frank thought, 'I'll bet she was a real beauty when she was younger. She sure knows what she's doing; her energy and friendliness are startling.' He found himself paying attention to how she worked and listening to her whenever she spoke. She seemed dedicated to helping her customers have an enjoyable meal. It suddenly dawned on him that one of the reasons she seemed so compelling to him was because she was treating all the customers in the same caring and respectful manner that he remembered Rose using.

"Could you stop that drumming," Brian said, "it's driving me nuts."

"Oh, sure, sorry. Old habits die hard you know. It used to drive my mother nuts too. I drummed my fingers whenever we played cards."

"Did you guys play cards a lot?"

"Yep; we played rummy mostly, but sometimes we'd play other games. My dad was one of the most competitive people I've ever known; God, how I loved to beat him."

"Sounds like fun, I guess."

"Do you ever play card games with your folks?"

"Not so much."

"When they meet up with us I can teach you; I'll bet your dad still remembers."

"Okay."

The bell under the heat lamp rang. Frank looked up, surprised to see two steak dinners sitting there already. Meg quickly brought them over. "Here you are gentlemen, two specials. Enjoy your meal. Is there anything else I can get for you?"

"Yes please," Frank answered, "could I have another biscuit?"

"Absolutely."

She walked toward the kitchen area singing out, "Oh Bert, can I have a couple of biscuits warmed up for table two."

Frank looked down at his dinner, and then glanced over to Brian. The steaks sat sizzling on the plates, steam rising from the vegetables and potatoes. The aroma of their food was enticing. "Now, this is more like it."

Brian, already placing a forkful of meat in his mouth muttered, "Yeah."

After a couple of minutes, Meg was back with a small plate that held two warmed biscuits. "Here you are. How are your steaks, okay?"

Brian replied, "Great." Frank, his mouth full, could only nod enthusiastically.

"Wonderful; is there anything else I can do for you?"

Frank swallowed and said, "I think we're good for now, thank you."

"No, thank you. Bert really works hard trying to please our customers and I appreciate your patience. Enjoy your meal. When you're done I'll come back and take your dessert order."

While they ate, Frank watched the waitress move from one table to another. 'She moves quickly and easily; she must have been an athlete at one time, she carries herself with such grace and poise.' Once when she reached up to secure a plate from the shelf he noticed her calves were strong and muscled, the definition clearly visible.

Thomas emerged from the kitchen pushing a tall metal rack with wheels that held about 20 or so pies. He had a pair of clear disposable gloves on and he started to unload the pies into the display case. As he placed pies on one of the shelves, Frank smiled and said to Brian, "There's your blueberry pie, Boyo."

"Sweet."

"Well, you're right there. Pies are sweet."

"Very funny. If they're half as good as this steak, we are in for a treat. This was a really good dinner, huh, Gramps?"

"Yes it was, Brian. Yes it was."

The last mouthful of food from Brian's dinner disappeared at about the same time that Meg walked by their table. "Can I take your plate, young man?" she asked.

"Yes, please."

"How was it?"

"It was great. You were right."

"I do get it right sometimes; I checked your ticket. Diane noted you wanted blueberry pie with a scoop of vanilla ice cream. Correct?"

"Yes. It's my favorite."

"Alrighty, then; that's what you'll get." Meg turned to Frank and added, "It looks like you're about ready for dessert too; what would you like, sir?"

"I'll have the same please, and a coffee."

"Comin' right up. Can I clear your plate as well?"

Frank looked down and realized that the only thing left on his plate was a small, grizzled piece of steak and part of a biscuit. "Sure, that'd be fine; thank you."

When Meg brought their dessert, Frank asked her a question that had been on his mind. "There sure seems to be quite a lot of pie in that display case. Are you really busy at dinner times?"

"Yes sir. It's still a little early yet, but we're going to get real busy, real soon."

"And you're shorthanded, right?"

Meg let out a long, soft sigh, "We are that. But, we'll get by, one way or another, we always do. Now, enjoy that pie; it's on us, remember. It's the least we can do."

"I'm sure we will," Frank replied, "it looks delicious."

Brian added, "It sure does."

Fresh, ripe, Oregon blueberries were suspended in a sugary blue filling and nestled in a flaky, buttery pie crust. The first few bites were enjoyed in silence with only an occasional satisfied hum escaping from Brian. Frank smiled as he remembered a young Robert humming whenever he ate something he'd really liked. The memory of those times when his own family was young brought a smile to Frank's face, followed by that old feeling of loss that still surfaced when he thought about his wife. 'Too young, you missed so much. We missed so much.'

Suddenly, he realized he'd been thinking about the Appetitto Shop, how busy they'd been at times and how Sonny had saved the day. 'Wait a second, we can help these guys, and it might even be fun. I know at the very least it'll be an interesting experience for Brian. I wonder if he'll want to help. It'd sure be cool if we do.'

"Hey, Brian," Frank spoke out. "I have an idea and I'd like you to hear me out before you make up your mind, okay?"

"Sure Gramps. Shoot."

"We're not in any particular hurry to get into camp. I've set up camp in the dark plenty of times. With a camper it's really pretty easy. I was thinking; if you wouldn't mind working for a little while we can help these people get through dinner. They're gonna get slammed and they're really shorthanded. We can make a real difference here and I'll bet you could earn a few dollars to boot. What do you think?"

"Aw, Gramps, I don't know anything about working in a restaurant. How much good will I be? Besides, they might not want our help."

"Good point, but we can at least offer. I'm sure that you wouldn't be asked to do anything you're not capable of. It'll be a great experience for you. Brian, some time or another everyone needs help. It's simple. It is. These people need help. When you're older, you'll look back and remember what you did. You'll remember, with pride, the times you connected with others. Now, we can easily go on the rest of our journey without another thought about Bert, Meg and Thomas and their customers, or we can choose to help them. And trust me, Boyo, if we decide to help it will be an experience you'll remember. Besides, it might just be fun."

"Gramps I'm ... not sure, but ... well, okay, let's do it."

Chapter Eighteen

As Brian sat and silently pondered his grandfather's proposal, he certainly wasn't thrilled. He didn't know anything about working in a restaurant. He'd never done anything other than an occasional odd job for his parents or a neighbor. He looked down at the last bit of pie on his plate and hoped the owner wouldn't want them to help. He pushed the pie from one side of the plate to the other before slicing it in half with his fork. He speared one bite and brought it to his mouth. The pie had been delicious, but either he was getting full or it just didn't taste as good anymore. He felt like he wanted to tell his grandfather he'd changed his mind and would much rather leave than stay, but when he looked up his grandfather smiled back with enthusiasm.

"Finish up, Boyo, and we will pay our bill and see what they say. Okay?"

"Yeah, sure Gramps."

Frank slid over to the end of the booth. He used his hand to steady himself and then stood up. As he walked over toward the register he reached into his pocket for his cash and looked over to where Meg was busy wrapping utensils in napkins. She glanced up and said, "How was everything? Pretty good, huh? Aren't you glad you stayed?"

"It was great. Best steak and pie I've had in a long time. And, yes, we are glad we stayed."

Meg totaled the check and took the money that Frank held toward her then quickly counted back the change and with a big smile added, "Thanks again for your patience, sir, and if you are ever passin' through this neck o' the woods again, please stop back. There are a lot of different pies, all freshly baked."

"Excuse me," Frank interrupted, "I would like to have a word with Bert, please."

Meg looked startled. She stopped as if in mid-thought and replied with a puzzled look on her face, "Bert is really busy right now and at the best of times he doesn't do all that well with customers when he's cooking. He usually lets me handle any complaints. I thought you said everything was okay, right?"

"Everything was fine Meg. I ... um ... well, my grandson and I would like to offer to help you get through dinner. We're not in a hurry to get anywhere and I used to work in a deli in New York when I was younger. At least, I can wash dishes. Brian here hasn't worked before and he's concerned that he might not be much help but we're willing to try, anyway." Frank shrugged as if it were no big deal. "Bert wouldn't need to pay me; I'm happy to help, but he might want to pay my grandson something for his time if that would be okay."

While Frank talked the expression on Meg's face went from bewilderment to astonishment. "Wow! That is such a nice thing for you to offer. Aren't you both so sweet! I guess I'd better go ask Bert and see what he says. I'll be right back." Meg gave Frank and Brian a huge smile and turned to walk to the kitchen.

Brian stole a glance at his grandfather and swore the old man was blushing. "Wow, did you see her face light up when she realized we were offering to help?"

"Yep."

Bert walked out from the kitchen smiling and drying his hands on a paper towel. He said, "Meg told me what you guys are willing to do and I really appreciate the offer, but are you sure?"

Frank returned Bert's smile, nodded his head and replied, "We would be happy to help in any way we can. I remember what it's like taking care of customers shorthanded. I also remember what having unexpected help can mean. I can do dishes and well, Brian here has never worked, but I think he'll be okay. He is a little nervous about this, but he's a fast learner and if you find something he can do I'm sure he'll be fine."

"We surely can use your help; there's no denying that. Sure, I'll be happy to pay both of you."

"Not for me," Frank answered, "I'm glad to pitch in. Just pay Brian; in a way it's his first job."

"Fine, thanks ... well all right, let's see ... okay, come on back to the kitchen; I'm in the middle of cooking some dinners."

Brian and Frank followed Bert back to the kitchen area. Brian was filled with curiosity since this was the first time he'd ever been in the kitchen of a restaurant. The cooking area was rather large and included a stainless steel gas stove with a grill, a black griddle, a commercial microwave oven and a large convection oven near the counter that fronted the dining room. This entire area was covered by exhaust hoods whose fans made a constant noise. The back area of the kitchen contained a long, stainless steel, three-station sink next to an imposing commercial dishwasher. A six-foot long, wheeled table with a wooden top stood in the center of the kitchen and to the left of the sink was another table that held an immense pile of dirty dishes. Thomas was busy chopping celery on the big table. He looked up briefly. There were three big stainless steel refrigerators; one was a walk in. More stainless shelves and wire racks held other appliances, spice containers, and some other plastic containers. There were two large garbage cans, both lined with plastic bags and both on wheels. One of these was near the table by the sink; one was on the other side of the stove.

Brian noticed steam rising from a large pot on the stove. Bert washed his hands twice, then went right over to the grill and used a long metal spatula to turn two chicken breasts before giving the pot a stir. He turned to Frank and said, "Those dishes need cleaning, let me show you how we do 'em." Bert moved across the kitchen to the sink area and took a dirty dish from the pile on the table. He cleaned it as he continued, "We use this sprayer to scrape the dishes as clean as possible, then we wash them in this first sink, which has soap in it. You dip the clean dish in this sink, which is a clear rinse, then into the last sink which contains a sanitizing solution. They are then placed in one of these racks to air dry." He finished by adding, "The dishwasher's broken so we have to clean them all by hand."

Frank replied, "We didn't have a dishwasher at the deli where I worked so 'by hand' is all I know anyway."

"You'll want to wear this rubber apron to stay dry and if you want gloves to put on we have these as well." Bert indicated a pair of heavy rubber gloves on the shelf that ran the length of the wall above the sink.

Frank took the apron and said, "I think I'll wash without the gloves first and see how that works, but I will wear this apron."

"Oh! I almost forgot, this sprayer, called a scraper, can shoot water all over the place if you don't aim it deep down into the sink. The overspray can get the floor pretty wet and I don't want anyone slipping. Our employees all have slip-proof work shoes. Please be careful."

"Understood."

Frank put on the apron, grasped the scraper in his right hand, a plate in his left and proceeded to imitate the steps Bert had just shown him. The scraper, a power spray head attached to a long flexible metal-covered hose, quickly removed the food left on the plate. "Wow," Frank said, "That's cool. We sure could have used this at the Appetitto."

"Where?" Bert asked.

"The deli where I worked."

"Oh." Bert turned his attention to Brian. "I think," he started, "we better have you help Meg. You can clear tables and do whatever else she needs done; I'm sure that will be good."

Bert said to Thomas, "With these guys helping, you can go on a break after all, but Thomas, please make it quick, okay?"

Thomas looked relieved and quickly agreed. "Sure Bert; is 20 minutes okay?"

"That'll be fine."

Bert washed his hands, and then moved back to the stove. He used a metal meat thermometer to check the temperature of the chicken and placed them on two plates, added some vegetables, checked the tickets and placed mashed potatoes on one plate and french fries on the other. He put the two plates on the window and rang the bell. Meg soon appeared to whisk the plates to the table. When she returned to get utensils and glasses ready for another table, Bert told her that Brian would be helping her. He added, "When Thomas returns from his break he'll help prep salads and desserts for the dining room."

Meg smiled at Brian, "So you're stuck with me, huh. Well, before we get really busy you'd better tag along and I'll try to get you ready."

"Yes, ma'am."

"Just call me Meg, okay, Brian?"

"Sure, Meg."

"So, let's see, you need a crash course on working in a restaurant. Where should I start? Okay, hand-washing discipline. When you work with food, it's essential that you wash your hands properly. If you use the bathroom you need to wash your hands before leaving the bathroom and then again before you return to work. You need to wash them long enough and thoroughly enough to kill all the germs that might be on your hands." She walked over to a small sink near the stove and said, "This is one of our hand-washing sinks; there are two back here and one up front. This is special anti-bacterial soap. You should turn on the water and get it warm." Meg demonstrated as she spoke, "Soap up and wash your hands really well; make sure you get under the fingernails with this brush. Fingernails should be well trimmed so dirt and germs can't be transferred to the food you might handle. Wash your hands for about 20 seconds or about as long as it takes you to sing the happy birthday song. You know that one, I'm sure. 'Happy Birthday to you, happy birthday to you, happy birthday happy birthday' ... got it?"

Brian nodded and when Meg was done washing her hands she waved them in front of a paper towel dispenser that automatically dispensed a single towel. She removed the towel and dried her hands. Brian moved up to the sink and imitated Meg.

While he washed his hands she continued, "If you touch anything that's not clean like garbage or dirty dishes, or not sanitized, you need to wash your hands again. When you start work you should do a double hand wash, so repeat the process again before you dry your hands. If you touch your face or hair, blow your nose, eat or smoke, or cough into your hand you have to double wash your hands." Meg pointed to a box of the plastic gloves before continuing, "Even if you're going to wear these food service gloves you need to wash your hands before you put them on. We want to make sure that the food we serve is not going to get a customer sick. Make sense?"

"Yes, of course."

"When you work in a restaurant you wash your hands a lot." She paused long enough to remember something else. "Along the same lines, we also need to make sure that the food we serve cannot be cross-contaminated. For example, that means that when the cook is preparing chicken using one of these plastic cutting boards, or any surface for that matter, the surface must be cleaned with a sanitizing solution before anything else is placed on it so germs from one food are not transferred to another." Meg pointed out a white plastic bucket. "These buckets contain washcloths in a solution of water and a little bleach. We test the solution from time to time to make sure it's still good. Every once in a while we change them out with fresh solution. Here, I'll show you. The bucket up front needs to be changed." Meg walked toward the front counter with Brian trailing behind.

"I like to keep some clean cloths handy to wipe down tables, this counter and any other surfaces that should be sanitized, including any surfaces a customer might touch." Meg kept up a constant stream of chatter as she went about her task. "We use cool water and just about a half-capful of bleach; there, that's done." Meg paused to see if Brian understood then added, "Okay, that table over there needs to be cleared and wiped, we'll use one of these—" she said, pointing to a fairly large black plastic tub, "—they're called cambros." Meg grabbed the cambro and a washcloth from the bucket and walked briskly over to the table. Without delay she started to place dishes, utensils and glasses into the tub, explaining as she went, "All the dirty dishes go back to the kitchen to be cleaned. It's our job to clear these tables quickly and get them clean, set, and ready for the next customers. Oh! And if there are any sharp knives or if you have to clean up some broken glass, we don't want the person washing the dishes to cut themselves when they reach in. We put the sharp knives on top, here, handles up and use a different bucket to clean up broken glass."

Brian watched as Meg finished putting the last of the dirty dishes into the tub. He picked up the washcloth and wiped down the table. Meg said, "Very good, now take these back to the kitchen and I'll wash my hands and set the table. Oh! Be careful when you turn that corner going into the kitchen, someone might be on the way out and we don't need an accident."

"Okay, Meg I'll be careful."

"Good boy, come right back; we have a lot more to cover."

Brian walked carefully with the tub. When he reached the table that held the dirty dishes he asked, "Bert, what should I do with these?"

"Just leave them there for now. We've got plenty of those tubs and until we make more of a dent in that pile of dirty dishes that'll be fine. If we ever get caught up you could help the dishwasher by stacking dishes."

Frank laughed and said, "I'll get caught up, you just wait and see."

Brian, seeing a chance to needle his grandfather, said, "There are three more tables that need to be cleared and if I don't miss my guess, I'll be bringing you dirty dishes all night long."

"So, you don't think I'll get caught up, huh. Well, we'll see about that."

True to his word Brian quickly returned again and again with more dirty dishes. Each time he added to the pile he mentioned to his grandfather that it was still a formidable collection. Frank just laughed and kept on washing. No sooner did Meg and Brian clear all the remaining tables then Meg said, "All right, we may have 15 or 20 minutes before we start getting busy; why don't you help with dishes while I finish up waiting on these customers."

Brian replied, "Sure thing." When he went back to the kitchen he said to Bert, "Meg said I should help with dishes until we get busy. What should I do?"

"Here, help your grandfather by taking the dishes from him after he sprays them. Wash them, rinse them, sanitize them, and then stack them in one of these racks."

"The racks seem to be getting kind of full, aren't they?" Brian observed.

"Yes, but Thomas will put the dry ones away as soon as he's back from break, which should be any minute now."

Brian did as instructed. He asked his grandfather how it was going and Frank answered, "Just fine, Boyo, there's nothing too complicated about washing dishes. How are things up front?"

"We have all the tables cleared and Meg is taking care of the people that are here."

Bert piped in from in front of the stove, "The dinner rush should begin any time now. Thanks again, guys, for your help. You don't know what it means to me ... to us."

Frank replied, "Not at all, Bert. We're happy to help."

When Thomas returned, he washed his hands twice before Bert told him to put the clean dishes away. Steadily the collection of dirty dishes dwindled to a more manageable size. Just when Brian thought they might even be getting close to getting caught up, Meg stuck her head around the corner and said, "Brian, we have more tables to clear."

Brian chuckled and said to his grandfather, "More dirty dishes for you, Gramps."

"Keep 'em comin', Boyo."

Meg had already started clearing one of the tables by the time Brian made it out to the dining room. Brian helped her finish it, and then took the tub to the next table to clear it. While he was doing this Meg used the washcloth to wipe the first table and dropped it on the table Brian was clearing. She greeted new guests. This time when Brian brought back the tub to the kitchen, Meg called back to Bert asking that someone get some salads ready. Bert agreed, but Thomas was still busy putting dishes away, so Bert showed Brian how to prep salads. First he had Brian wash his hands again before getting a dozen salads ready for the dinner rush.

Bert seemed to like the progress of the work. He kept talking constantly despite being extremely busy cooking and getting plates ready. "If you ever do get another job in a restaurant Brian, there are other really important things you should know. For instance, do you see those heat lamps there?" Bert continued without waiting for an answer, "Once food is cooked it's important to keep it hot. The temperature should never fall below 140 degrees. Cold food should be kept at 40 degrees or less."

Brian finished with the salads just as Thomas got the last of the dry dishes stacked. Thomas said to Brian, "These go in the refrigerator up front; grab some and I'll show you." With this done, Thomas returned to the kitchen. Brian noticed another table to be cleared. The people who had been there were at the register paying their bill, so he grabbed a tub and started right in getting the table ready. It was a pattern that would repeat itself many times during the course of the evening. Meg came over with fresh place settings and told Brian he was doing a good job. She added, "Brian, we are now officially in dinner time; it won't slow down till after eight. I'm going to need you to help me wait on tables as well as clear and set. Let's take it one table at a time. Pay close attention and I'll do my best to make it as easy as possible on you. Okay?"

Brian looked around at the steadily filling dining room and swallowed. To Meg he replied, "Okay Meg, I'll do my best."

"That's all any of us can do, Brian. You'll be fine, just fine."

"I hope so."

Meg went back to check on four customers seated at a table near the window. Since they were ready, she took their orders. Turning toward the kitchen she said to Brian, "I'll need four waters, a Pepsi, and a coffee for that table. Here's what we do next; the order is attached to this ticket wheel and I'll let the cook know there is a new order up." Meg matched her action to her words by ringing the small bell and announcing in what Brian thought was a somewhat official voice, "Order up."

"Then," she said, "we need to get their drinks right over to them. Fast, efficient and friendly service is part of the Diner's Bill of Rights."

"What's that?"

"A few years ago Bert found this Diner's Bill of Rights on the Internet. It was more for fancy restaurants, you know, that serve wine and take reservations, and it had like 20 things listed that a diner in a restaurant should be able to expect. Well, anyway, Bert shortened it to fit any basic place, like this one. A diner in a restaurant has the right to get clean, healthy food prepared the way they want it, served with hospitality and in a reasonable amount of time. That, in a nutshell, is the Diner's Bill of Rights."

"That makes sense. If you get all that in a restaurant, I guess you'd be happy."

"Our goal here is to do a little more than that. We want to delight each customer with every aspect of their visit every time they visit. That's why Bert was so nervous about being shorthanded tonight. He thought we were going to let some customers down. Lucky for us, you and your grandfather happened along. Now, it looks like we'll be okay."

Chapter Nineteen

An older man sitting by himself at the counter asked, "Hey son, can I get some steak sauce, please?"

Brian looked up from the table he was clearing and replied with a smile, "Yes, sir, right away." He quickly finished putting the last of the dirty dishes into the tub, left the washcloth on the table and brought the dishes into the kitchen. "Hey, Gramps, here's some more dirty dishes for you." For the last hour or so, the restaurant had been busy. A steady stream of customers had kept Meg and Brian on their toes. During that time, Brian's main job had been clearing, wiping and setting tables. Occasionally, he was asked to help carry drinks or food to a table for a larger group of diners. Whenever Brian brought back more dishes he announced it to his grandfather. At first, Frank would laugh and make a funny remark, but this time his grandfather was strangely quiet. Brian noticed that Bert and Thomas also were silent. On the way back to the tables he grabbed two different kinds of steak sauces and brought them to the guest. "Here you are, sir. Is there anything else?"

"That's it for now, thanks."

Brian replied with a phrase he'd heard Meg say a lot, "Enjoy your meal."

Returning to the table he'd been clearing, Brian finished wiping it and was setting it when Meg walked by with a tray of food. She beamed a big smile at him and said, "You're doin' great, Brian. I left two plates on the window for this order. Would you wash your hands and get them right away and bring 'em to the table?"

"Sure thing, Meg."

As Brian turned from the sink to get the plates, a burst of laughter came from the kitchen. The older guest who had requested the steak sauce looked up from his meal and said to Brian, "Sounds like someone is having fun back there."

Brian replied, "It sure does." He wondered what might have been so funny. The plates under the heat lamps were hot, but not so hot that Brian couldn't hold onto them, and soon they were delivered to the table. Meg said, "Thank you, Brian." She nodded over to one of the large tables where the guests were just getting up to leave and added, "I'll take their check. Please clear that table next."

Brian responded, "WHY SOITENLY!" which brought a quick smile from both Meg and the old gentleman. Brian filled the tub quickly and brought it back to the kitchen. He announced, "Here's some more dirty dishes for you, Gramps."

Frank looked up from the sink where he was still working steadily and replied, "Great, just what I needed, more dishes. I need more dirty dishes like Custer needed another Indian." Brian and Thomas both laughed at his remark but Bert turned from the stove and in a very serious tone said, "Frank I'm sure you don't know this, but I'm part Indian. I find those kinds of remarks to be degrading." He said no more but stood waiting as if expecting something from Frank. Brian stopped laughing and studied his grandfather. Frank's face changed from a grin to one of concern. He faced Bert and started to fluster an apology, "Gee Bert, I'm sorry … I, um, didn't mean to …"

Bert interrupted Frank with loud sudden laughter, "I got you that time! Ha, ha, ha … I am part Indian, but I just wanted to see your face when I said that. I got you good."

Brian watched his grandfather's face turn red in confusion before breaking into a broad grin. He laughed then, as loudly as Bert had, and through his laughter said, "Yes Bert, you certainly did get me, you sure did." Thomas and Brian joined in the laughter until after a short time Bert wiped a tear from his face and turned to the hand-wash sink saying, "Ah! That was good. I haven't laughed like that in a long time. Okay, back to work."

Returning to the dining room, Brian noticed that the older gentleman was smiling at him. "Somebody back there has a quirky sense of humor."

Brian replied, "Actually, they're a pair of nuts back there."

"It's good to hear laughter."

Meg, meanwhile, had finished pouring coffee and returned to the counter with two empty coffee pots. She said to Brian, "Hey kiddo, do you know how to make coffee?"

"Well, not really."

"Okay then, let me show you. Here are the filters; here's where we keep the coffee. They are in these pre-measured pouches. You put a filter into one of these brew baskets, open the pouch, pour the coffee into the filter, slide the basket into the brewer, make sure the pot is right below and hit this green button. Got that?"

"Sure, Meg."

"Okay then, brew another pot, but make it a decaf. You'll use one of these pouches; see, it says decaffeinated."

"Okay."

Once Brian finished brewing the decaf, he looked around to see what needed doing next. The tables were almost all full and for the moment, none needed to be cleared. He brought the tub back to the kitchen with only a few dirty dishes. Bert was busy cooking and his grandfather had made steady progress on the dishes. Thomas worked closely with Bert getting orders filled and ready for Meg. Brian returned to the dining room. Despite being busy, Meg had found the time to set the last table, so Brian spent a little time just standing near the end of the counter watching Meg move from table to table. In most cases, she asked if everything was okay or if the guests wanted something. Sometimes, she just looked at the people at the table and when all seemed okay, moved on without a word. The dining room buzzed with the sound of conversation punctuated by clinking dinnerware. It seemed to Brian a warm and happy place.

"Hey, son, can I ask you a question?" It was the older man again.

Brian looked at him and suddenly realized that the old man bore a striking resemblance to Mr. Bartley, his freshman English teacher, only older. He smiled and answered with something his grandfather had said to him once, "You just did."

The man laughed and continued, "I did, indeed. Okay then, another question. What kind of pie would you recommend?"

"Well, I've only had the blueberry, but it was great! Warmed up with a scoop of vanilla ice cream; it was great."

"Sounds good, would you bring me one?"

"I'll let Meg know. Yes sir."

Meg was at the register ringing up guests so Brian waited for a chance to tell her of the old man's request. She answered, "Fine, go tell Thomas. He'll get it ready for you and then go ahead and bring it to him. Okay?"

"Sure."

Brian had just delivered the pie when three groups of customers entered the restaurant. Meg seated the couple that came in first, then the larger group at the bigger table. Now, all the tables were full. The last four were faced with a decision to wait or leave. Meg looked around the dining room and stated, "It will be about 10 to 15 minutes before we'll be able to seat you." While they discussed this among themselves, she turned to Brian and said, "Okay kid, first we're going to need drinks brought right out for those tables, then after we get them settled in we'll need the next available table cleared and set. Go fill eight glasses with water and load them on a tray."

Brian replied, "Okay."

He went quickly to the counter area, prepared a tray and filled eight glasses with ice and water. He placed them in the center of the tray, the way Meg had instructed. Then he firmly gripped the edges of the tray, picked it up and started toward the tables. As he began to move from behind the counter, he noticed some movement on his right. Meg was quickly leaving the kitchen with onion rings and they were about to collide! Brian tried to swing the tray out of the way before Meg ran into it, but in doing so the waters shifted on the tray and soon all eight glasses went crashing to the floor. Brian stood there for a second not knowing what to do. All of the diners looked up at the sound of the crashing glass. He felt embarrassed. Meg paused for a second and said, "I'll be right back Brian. It's okay. We'll get it cleaned up in a jiffy."

The old man at the counter looked up from his pie and added, "You almost saved it, son. It wasn't entirely your fault."

Before Brian could reply, Frank and Thomas were both out from the kitchen. They immediately began to clean up the mess. They were soon joined by Meg, who said to Brian, "I'm sorry, kiddo, I know better than to hurry like that. Fill up eight more glasses and let's get back on track. Thomas and your grandfather will finish cleaning this up."

Although Brian felt embarrassed about dropping the tray and nervous about doing it again, Meg's matter-of-fact attitude helped him regain his composure. He filled new glasses and delivered them to the tables. When he was finished he took the tray into the kitchen. He felt a need to get away from the dining area. He imagined everyone was laughing at him. Bert greeted him as he entered the kitchen, "Brian, please don't worry about that. Mistakes happen; mistakes are okay as long as we learn from them." For emphasis Bert placed his hand on Brian's forearm then added, "Do you know Thomas Edison was asked once how he felt about the ten thousand failed experiments that led to the invention of the light bulb. Do you know what he said?"

Brian shrugged and shook his head no.

"Edison said ... I haven't failed; I've just found ten thousand ways that won't work. Think about that, Brian. We learn from our mistakes." Bert paused, smiled at Brian then asked, "Okay, what could you have done differently that might have helped you to avoid that?"

"I don't know," Brian replied glumly, "maybe not be in so much of a hurry."

Bert nodded his head in agreement and said, "Very good. Not be in so much of a hurry. Here's another quote I really like, 'be quick but don't hurry'."

Frank paused in his dishwashing and turned to observe Bert talk to Brian. He smiled and chimed in, "That's John Wooden. I quote him all the time. That's one of my favorites. 'Be quick but don't hurry,' that's great, Bert."

Bert agreed, "That's right; it is John Wooden. Good stuff, huh, Frank?"

"You bet."

Turning back to Brian, Bert continued, "In a restaurant you are part of a team. Being part of a team means that sometimes you are there to help others, while sometimes your teammates are there for you. In life you earn the respect of others by your actions. Watching you work tonight and seeing all the things you have done so well has earned my respect and I know Meg feels the same way. Mistakes are just opportunities to learn. Now, why don't you take a 10-minute break; drink some water and settle down. We'll manage okay for a little while without you. Okay?"

"Sure ... thanks."

Brian grabbed a glass from the clean dishes and began to pour himself a drink as Bert had suggested. He noticed a stool in the corner and decided to sit there. As he began to relax, Meg came into the kitchen with a big smile on her face. First she said to Bert, "Hey Bert, guess who just walked into the restaurant?" Without waiting for Bert to reply she answered her own question with, "Diane. Diane is back; we've got the rest of dinner covered." Meg then came over to where Brian sat on the stool. She looked into his eyes and smiled. "Hey kiddo, you know that old man at the counter?"

"Yeah," Brian answered with a nod.

"Well, he just left, but before he did he wanted me to tell you that he felt like you provided him with great service and he said he couldn't remember enjoying a meal in a restaurant more. He left a very big tip. You made his day, he said. You were great."

Brian felt better immediately and said, "Thank you Meg, but aren't the tips for you?"

"You earned a share of the tips, and you'll get it. Now you just rest a moment until we get back to a more normal shift routine, and what with dinner almost over and Diane back, we can probably cut you and your grandfather loose."

Brian looked at the clock when Meg said that dinner was almost over and was startled to see that it was a little after seven-thirty. They had been working steadily since before five but the time seemed to have passed so quickly that Brian would not have guessed that it was anywhere near that late.

Diane came back to the kitchen to wash her hands and said to Frank, "Meg told me what you and your grandson have done and I can't thank you enough. You wouldn't believe how bad I felt leaving Bert and Thomas so shorthanded."

Frank replied, "Everyone needs help from time to time. It was a pleasure to be of service and to get to know Bert."

After his short break, Brian resumed his duties of clearing, wiping and setting tables. With Diane back, the two waitresses were able to easily keep up with the tables. They took turns at the register ringing up the guest tickets, taking payments and giving change. It was obvious to Brian that they were used to working together. Near the end of dinner the number of new guests slowed down quite a bit as did the number of dirty dishes Brian brought back for his grandfather to clean; soon, Frank was caught up.

The tub contained only a few dishes on Brian's last trip to the kitchen. As he set it down on the table, Bert turned from the stove to speak. "Frank, I can't thank you and Brian enough for what you have done for us here tonight. Without your help we never would've been able to keep up with the guests we had. As it turned out, we were able to do a good job and send most of them out of here happy. On top of that I haven't laughed that hard in a long time." He turned to Brian and added, "And you, young man, you did great. You sure caught on quickly and worked well and steadily. You more than earned this." Bert held some money in his hand and extended it toward Brian. Brian smiled and took the money with a feeling of pride.

Bert continued, "Now Frank, I know you said we didn't have to pay you, but you sure did clean a boatload of dirty dishes and I can't send you out of here empty-handed. I want you to take one of my specialty pies along on your camping trip. It's a hazelnut pie I'm almost famous for. It's like a pecan pie, but nuttier."

"Thank you Bert, I'd be honored." Frank smiled and clasped Bert's hand in a hearty handshake.

Meg entered the kitchen at this moment. Flashing a radiant smile she said, "I hear you guys are getting ready to take off. I wanted to give Brian his share of the tips and tell you both how happy we were to work with you. You really helped us get through a tough time and I appreciate just how much you did." She handed

Brian his tips and stepped up to give him a warm hug. Turning to Frank she added, "Tonight was great. Your willingness to help was tremendous and you have a great kid here; I want you to know that."

Frank smiled and replied, "I know; he's a good kid." She stood looking at Frank for a moment. She leaned forward as if to shake his hand but with a shrug and a smile Meg stepped up to Frank and gave him a hug as well.

Frank seemed startled by Meg's gesture. He returned the hug awkwardly.

Meg leaned into Frank and whispered a few short words to him that Brian couldn't quite hear. He watched carefully for a response from his grandfather but Frank simply smiled back at Meg and nodded his head yes.

They left the restaurant. Brian walked with his grandfather, who carried his pie, across the parking lot to their truck. He remembered going into the restaurant only a few hours before. Now, as they left, he felt as if something important had happened to him; he felt like he was somehow different. He was tired, very tired in fact, but felt satisfied with himself and happy.

Chapter Twenty

"Wow! That sure was amazing, huh, Boyo?"

"Yeah, Gramps, it sure was, but, I'm beat. It's been a long day."

"Well, you just rest a while. In fact, why don't you take a short nap? Frenchglen, where we turn off to Fish Lake, is just about an hour or so south of here. When we get there I'll wake you up so you can see the town and get a little familiar with the area."

"Okay, Gramps … sounds great." With that, Brian put on a baseball cap, pulled the brim down over his eyes, as he saw his grandfather do the day before, and settled down into the corner of the cab.

Frank was glad that Brian wanted to sleep. He thought the boy had worked hard and done remarkably well, considering he'd never worked at a restaurant before. He also felt fortunate that Brian had worked with someone as expert as Meg. He'd watched as she instructed Brian and directed his activity. Meg impressed Frank with her professionalism, her friendliness and her kindness. He was also glad Brian wanted to sleep for another reason; Frank wanted to think. In his life, whenever he'd been faced with a complicated or powerful situation, Frank had learned to calm himself and review the events before making up his mind. He'd been a little too quick to judge when he was younger. Now, he liked to analyze things more carefully; he knew things were rarely black or white and he'd learned to look for the gray.

When Meg had hugged him as they were leaving she'd said three simple words to him: 'Enjoy your life.' She said these words differently than when she'd said to diners, 'Enjoy your meal.' The way she said it caught him by surprise. She had stressed all the words with perhaps a little more emphasis on the word 'your'. It was said in such an unusual way that to Frank it seemed to trigger

a strong emotional response. He needed to think about the effect
her words had on him. Also interesting to Frank was Bert, who
seemed somehow familiar even though they'd never met before. The
way he joked around and approached things made Frank think they
shared a lot in common. He believed that if given the chance he
and Bert could be friends. The entire experience compelled careful
consideration. Frank settled into driving, so deep in thought that
the roadside terrain barely made an impression upon him until the
lengthening shadows of dusk prompted him to turn on his lights.

Off to the right, the last of the day's sun fell behind the rimrock.
It peeked through the occasional canyon or draw; golden sunlight
illuminating rocks, sagebrush and juniper whose shadows stretched
far along the ground. Frank noticed several deer standing in a field
about 200 yards from the road and as he returned his attention to
driving, saw a jackrabbit scurry across the road just in front of his
truck. 'That was sure close. You wascally wabbit, a little slower and
you would've been road kill.'

Frank drove awhile before realizing that he was feeling tired. He
switched the air conditioner on to 'fresh air.' The pervading smells
of Eastern Oregon, juniper and sage, filled the cab. He remembered
back to the last time he'd camped at Fish Lake. The kids were still
young enough to be all fun and little drama. Moira was still alive
and they were in love. The days before her chemotherapy treatments
began were the best of his life. He still yearned for the love and
happiness they'd shared as a family. Now his children were grown
with children of their own. The best he could hope for was the
occasional visit or vacation. That was why Frank had so looked
forward to this camping trip. Not only did he get to spend some
time with his family, but he got to do so in a place where he had
forged such fond memories.

But the memories of his earlier life caused Frank pain as
well. At places along the North Umpqua where he and his wife

had stopped early in their marriage, memories flooded his mind, reminding him of his loss. He worried about how he would feel revisiting another place where he and Moira had shared such good times. 'Of course,' he thought, 'Brian's company provides a bright spot.' And what a bright spot the boy was! Cheerful, happy and inquisitive, Brian reminded Frank of what it was like to be young again. As his thoughts turned toward the present, he laughed at himself for being so melodramatic. He chided himself, 'just be grateful for what you have, old man, and make the most of what you've got left.' Then unbidden, a thought surfaced that made him reflect again on those three words whispered in his ear less than an hour ago, "Enjoy your life."

A short while later Brian shifted in his seat. Frenchglen was only a few miles away, so Frank decided to wake the boy up. He reached over, gently shook his shoulder and said, "Hey there, Boyo, time to wake up. We'll be gettin' into Frenchglen shortly."

"Huh? Oh, okay."

"You sure slept well. The town is coming up in less than five minutes so you'd better wake up or you'll miss it."

Brian, still trying to rouse himself, answered with a somewhat flip, "Wouldn't want to do that."

Frank laughed, "And you wouldn't want to sleep too long now or you might have a tough time gettin' to sleep later."

"I don't think that will be a problem, Gramps. I feel really tired."

"I'll bet you do, son ... I'm sure you'll sleep well tonight."

Brian looked out the window at the side of the road and rubbed his face. "It's dark. What time is it?"

Frank laughed before answering, "It's NOW, of course; and, it's time for you to see Frenchglen in all its splendor. The road to Fish Lake is just on the other side of town."

They passed a sign that informed the travelers they were entering Frenchglen, but Brian saw only a few houses, a store and an ancient hotel that looked like it was transplanted from an old Western movie. Frank slowed and turned onto a small road on the left.

Brian exclaimed, "Wait a minute! That was it. That was Frenchglen?"

Frank nodded yes, his laughter serving as all the reply he could muster.

"You woke me up for that?"

Any reply Frank might have made was quickly forgotten when two deer stepped in front of the truck. He stepped firmly on the brake, all the while hoping that either the deer would get out of the way or he'd been going slowly enough to stop in time. Precisely when he thought that hitting one of them was inevitable, the closest deer sprang into the underbrush. The other, a large buck, simply turned his head toward the truck as Frank and Brian came to a complete stop. Only feet from the truck, he turned and walked off in the same direction the other deer had gone.

"Well, I'll be damned! Brian, did you see that buck?"

"He just stood there. We almost hit him and he just stood there."

"And did you see that rack?"

"Did I? It was huge!"

"Yes it was. He had at least five points on each side and the width of his antlers ... Wow!"

"Why did he just stand there, Gramps?"

"Shit if I know, Brian. Who knows what goes through the mind of a deer? I'm just glad I didn't hit him."

"That's for sure. Anyway, I'm awake now."

"I really didn't want you to nap too long, Brian. Once we get into camp we'll clear out the camper, just like we did at Whitehorse Falls, and get right to bed. I'm tired myself. Tomorrow, after breakfast, we have camp to set up, including the tent, the camper and a few other things we'll need when the rest of the gang gets here. I also wanted you to see how this road leads to the campground."

"Okay, Gramps."

"So now, please get out the map and I'll turn this cab light on." Frank matched his actions to his words and flipped on the light.

Brian responded by pulling out the map from where he'd pushed it between the console and his seat. He unfolded it.

Frank reached over, pointed to the road on the map and said, "Right here after we cross the Blitzen River the asphalt ends. Then we'll be on gravel. Towing a boat limits how fast we can drive on gravel, so it will take us about an hour or so to get there."

"It doesn't look that far, Gramps."

"No, it's only 17 or 18 miles."

Frank turned off the cab light before moving on. They came to a small bridge with a sign that read Blitzen River. The river looked no bigger than a stream. As he'd remembered, the road turned to gravel. Frank drove at less than 30 miles an hour. Almost immediately the road showed signs of severe washboarding. The gravel formed a continuous series of small ridges that made the truck shake and vibrate. Brian had never seen anything like it and asked his grandfather what caused it. Frank explained that over time, traffic on a gravel road forms those ridges. The more traffic using the road, the worse it got until a road crew would drive a big truck with a fixed blade on the front to smooth it out. "They must be getting set to blade this road soon, because this is as bad as I've ever seen."

Brian answered with a voice he allowed to be influenced by the vibration of the truck as it shook to the washboarding, "I…I… I … see…see…see … Gra…aaa…mmps."

Frank chuckled and drove on. In a few places the road seemed to be smoother and at these times Frank sped up to take advantage.

Frenchglen

When the road got particularly bad he slid over to the other side of the road trying to find the best route. Nothing seemed to work for long and they sat silently for a time. After 10 or 15 minutes headlights coming toward them prompted Frank to slow down. When they passed each other, they were momentarily blinded by the dust kicked up by the other truck.

"Wow, that truck sure is stirring up a lot of dust, huh, Gramps."

"Yes Brian. I'll bet we are too."

Brian looked in his side view mirror and through the dim light saw that yes indeed, they were leaving a dense ribbon of dust behind them as well. "We are."

Frank remembered that the air intake was set to fresh air. He reached over to change it. He explained to Brian the cab could be kept somewhat dust-free using the recycled air setting on the air conditioning. "The fine dust of Eastern Oregon is one of the things you'll have to get used to, Boyo; it's everywhere this time of year."

Frank had been paying close attention to the road ahead. They had crossed a couple of cattle guards, which were short metal bridges that prevented cattle from using the road to move from one field to another. This suggested the presence of cattle as well as the possibility of wildlife crossing in front, so he watched carefully. After a while, he noticed small trees with white trunks lining the road. Pointing them out to his grandson, he explained, "Brian, those trees with the white trunks are aspen, also known as quaking aspen. As I recall, they are one of the signs we're getting closer to the campground. They only grow at certain elevations."

The truck climbed steadily. Before too long, the sign that Frank had been waiting for announced their arrival at Fish Lake. He slowly pulled up to the campground visitor's area. The camp regulations were posted under a wooden roof. The various fees and a map of the campground with each campsite numbered provided orientation. Frank studied the map for a minute then turned to Brian. Pointing to the map, he said, "I seem to remember that these campsites were bigger and better suited for group campers. But if I remember right they were not all that easy to find. The side road into them starts over by this outhouse." He moved his finger to the left and continued, "We camped here before in this section."

"I hope we find a good spot soon; I'm tired."

"Let's go see."

Frank drove into the campground. They approached the place where the side road was supposed to be and had they not been purposely looking for it might well have missed it. Frank pulled the rig over to the side of the main roadway and turned the truck off. "Brian, I want to check this little road. In case it's not the right one, I don't want to run the risk of getting stuck in a tight spot with the boat. Would you open the glove box and hand me the flashlight that's in there, please? I'll take a short walk. Do you want to stay here or come along?"

"I'll come along, Gramps. I wouldn't mind stretching my legs."

Lined with juniper and sagebrush the little road soon entered a grove of aspen which led them into a series of large campsites. The first campsite was occupied but all the rest were available. Frank did a quick survey of the open campsites and found one that he liked. He explained to Brian, "This one looks good. There's a good spot for a tent, the fire pit is in a good central location and we can drive right through it either with or without the boat. These aspen will provide a degree of privacy, shade and may serve as a windbreak. Yep, this is really good. Let's go back to the registration box and sign in."

As at Whitehorse Falls and Chickahominy Reservoir, registration and payment were fairly easy and soon Frank drove the truck into their campsite. They unhitched the boat and pulled it out of the way. Frank started to unload the contents of the camper, while Brian walked up to the outhouse. When he returned, Brian grabbed the last few items, then helped Frank cover them with the tarp.

Frank looked around and said, "This is a nice campsite; I can't wait to see it in the daylight. In the meantime let's get to bed."

Brian sighed and added, "Bed sounds good."

Chapter Twenty-One

Frank woke up slowly before he became aware that the only sound he heard was a continuous faint rustling. Warm in his sleeping bag, he wondered, 'what's making that sound?' The sunlight streaming through the window above the sink told him that it was well after daybreak. He'd slept well. He felt rested and stretched lazily before realizing the need for a short walk to the outhouse. Pushing his bedding aside, he sat up. A hand dangled from the upper bed; Brian was still asleep. Frank dressed quietly, all the while wondering.

He opened the door and stepped out of the camper. Of course! A slow steady breeze blew through the aspen; each leaf was a fluttering flag. Countless leaves shimmered in the sunshine and flapped in the wind, each playing a part in the symphony. 'This sure is a nice spot,' Frank thought as he walked to the outhouse.

By the time he returned, the wind had died. The leaves now hung motionless. Frank stood at the entrance of their campsite. It offered plenty of room for the camper, a tent, both vehicles and the little portable gazebo he had along for shade. He tried to see it with the camper set up in one place, the tent in the other. 'Or maybe,' he thought, 'the tent would work better back in the trees over there and the camper here.' Frank decided to wait awhile before making up his mind. In the meantime, he stretched for several minutes, then pulled out a camp chair from the boat and waited for Brian to wake up.

After Brian got up, the pair ate breakfast in the camper and discussed their plans for the day. They stepped from the camper into bright sunshine. Frank explained to Brian where and why he thought the tent would work best. "This spot offers a little afternoon shade from these taller trees; the entrance will face away from the sun as well. The camper, I think, works best here and we can push the boat trailer over there, next to where the campsite meets the road. Anyway, we need to set up camp before we can have any fun, so let's get to it."

The camper stood supported by two wooden braces in addition to its jacks, which freed up the truck. With Brian's help, the tent was set up and the gazebo assembled but not staked down. Frank explained, "I want to see this spot about mid-afternoon before we plant this thing. As far as the rest of our set-up chores are concerned, well, we'll get 'em done later. What would you say to a walk?"

"Sounds good to me. What about fishing?"

"We'll get some fishin' in toward evening. First though, we've got a few things that need to get done as far as camp is concerned, like get water. Plus, we have to launch the boat."

"Okay Gramps, whatever you say."

Brian walked quietly beside his grandfather as they approached the road that led to the south end of Fish Lake. They turned right, onto the road that wound in and around the campsites at this end of the lake. The lake itself was not yet clearly visible but Brian could see an occasional patch of blue through the trees as they made their way down the road.

"This is the main highway of the campground, Boyo." Frank explained, "It connects the south end of the campground to the north end. This loop provides access to these campsites and there's another like it on the other side."

Every step they took kicked up a fine dust around their shoes. Tire tracks and footprints were easily discernable on the road.

Frank pointed to a set of prints on the side of the road, "Those are deer tracks, Brian. It looks like a doe and her fawn walked though here sometime last night."

"How can you tell that, Gramps?"

"Well, see these tracks are bigger than these, right?"

"Yeah."

"You can tell it's a doe, 'cause bucks have two little points that would be right here." Frank bent over and with his finger made two dots in the dust at the back of one of the hoof prints. "Bucks have what're called dew claws that leave a distinctive print. I'm assuming the smaller deer is a fawn that's still with its mother and they look fairly fresh; see how the edges of the print haven't yet collapsed. Deer are, for the most part nocturnal, they eat and move at night, so I'm guessing these were made last night or maybe this morning, but with people camped here I would imagine they moved through at night."

"Oh, that makes sense. You sure know a lot of stuff, Gramps. How did you learn that?"

"A friend of mine likes to hunt and I've gone out with him on a few scouting trips before hunting season. I always like to learn new things and so, in my lifetime, I have gathered quite a bit of interesting stuff." Frank said the word stuff in such a way as to indicate amusement at Brian's use of the word.

Brian chuckled back and replied, "The more stuff the better, huh?"

"Only if you can recall it and use it when you need it, Brian, otherwise it's just excess baggage."

Brian looked up and noticed that they were leaving the aspen behind. In front of them the far hillside lay covered in a carpet of sage brush and juniper with an occasional rock outcropping. Off to the right, he saw a dirt road that wound its way up and around the far slope. An empty campsite to their left looked well worn with use but clean. A small pile of firewood sat next to the fire pit. The next few campsites were taken but no people were in sight. As they turned toward the lake Brian noticed movement on the right. Glancing over in that direction he was surprised to see a large bird taking off from a rock about halfway up the hillside. It beat its wings three or four times and circled above the campground.

Frank exclaimed, "That's a red-tailed hawk! It's probably looking for a meal. They sure are pretty, aren't they?"

"Yes, they are."

"Keep your eyes open. I'll bet you'll see some eagles too."

"That would be sweet."

The water of Fish Lake reflected perfectly the brilliant blue of the sky. Large, white clouds floated through the air and were reflected in the lake as bright spots on the water. The lake itself was not big; it looked no more than 500 or 600 yards long and maybe 200 yards wide. Somewhat oval in shape, Fish Lake sat nestled between ridges to the west and east, with an almost continuous growth of aspen on the west side. The east slope was for the most part bare of trees except for a small grove of aspen that grew in a ravine on the northeast side of the lake. As Brian stood looking at Fish Lake for the first time, he wasn't impressed with its size. However, the quiet combined with the sense of solitude led him gradually to a deep feeling of peacefulness.

Brian stood as still as he could. He felt a slight breeze wash over him as he took in the view. The water rippled ever so slightly, the tiny waves broken only by an occasional trout upsetting the surface. For the moment, there was no sound save for the distant barking of a dog. Finally he spoke in a hushed tone, "It sure is pretty Gramps, but it's a lot smaller than I imagined it to be."

"Yep, it is small, but before we're done with this trip, Boyo, I'll bet you'll have some good memories of the place." Frank paused before continuing, "In fact, it's so small that we'll have to row. Motors of any kind, even my little trolling motor, are not permitted on Fish Lake."

"How will we troll?"

Frank laughed, "Why, the old fashioned way of course," he then added in song, "row, row, row your boat ... gently on the lake."

"Okay, okay, I get the picture."

"Let's go get some water and I'll show you the rest of the campground. Okay?"

"Fine with me, Gramps."

After walking back to their campsite, Frank threw a blue seven-gallon water container into the back of the pickup. Turning left onto the access road, he drove leisurely along the west ridge above the lake. Brian tried to catch a glimpse of the lake through the aspen. Frank took a right fork that descended toward the lake. "This road leads to the boat ramp over there," Frank indicated with a nod of his head toward Brian's side of the truck, "and loops around the campsites at this end."

As they drove slowly through the campground, Brian remained silent. A marshy meadow sat in the middle ringed by campsites, which all seemed to be taken. Tents occupied most of these campsites but no campers were in sight. They turned away from the lake and started to ascend toward the north end of the campground. On the passenger side the campsites seemed bigger. These were occupied by trailers, campers or motor homes. Frank explained, "These spots offer nice, big driveways but the ground is not that flat. The best tent sites are behind us down by the lake. See that spot right there?" He pointed to a campsite occupied by a trailer. "We camped there when your Dad was just 10 years old and Mary was six. That was a fun trip. Those trees sure look bigger than I remember them being. Ah, yes, time flies."

Brian looked carefully at the campsite as they drove by, trying to imagine his Dad at 10 and his Aunt Mary at six. "What did you guys do for fun?"

"Same thing we're gonna do this time; we'll fish, sightsee, hike and whatever else seems like fun. Camping way out here, there's not much else."

Frank seemed intent on recognizing a landmark ahead. "The water pump should be right up here," he said, "About where that hut is." He pointed to a small structure that had a solar panel on the roof. "Wait a second," he said as they came even with the small building, "this must be it. They used to have an old, red hand pump here to supply water to the camp. Looks like they modernized things a bit. The well now has a solar-powered electric pump. See the spigot there on the side?"

"Yeah Gramps, the ground is wet under it."

Frank's guess turned out to be correct and they soon had all the water their container could hold. "That old hand pump was kind of quaint. You know the type; where you have to pump it awhile, prime the pump, before you get any water. I was looking forward to seeing you pump the water by hand, Boyo, but they did make it easier, I guess."

On the way back to their camp, Frank drove into the boat ramp's parking area. "This is the boat ramp," he said as they pulled in, "and right over there is the dock. We can beach the boat here on this gravelly beach, tie it up to the dock or beach it on the other side of the lake. I think since we're camped on the other side, I'm leaning toward beaching it there." The dock to which Frank referred was a short distance south of the boat landing; the beach was north of it. A young boy stood on the bank above the beach throwing rocks into the lake.

"When are we going to put the boat in the water, Gramps?"

"How 'bout now?"

"Sure. Why not?"

"Okay then, let's go."

Within a matter of minutes, they had driven back to their campsite, hitched up the boat, added the oars and two life preservers.

Frank placed a small tool box in the boat and said, "That's all we need for now. Let's get going."

Frank soon had the boat in the water. A long rope tied to the bow allowed him to pull the boat over to the dock. Frank looked things over and said, "Okay then, Brian, you drive the truck and trailer back up to camp. Be careful ... I'll row over to that little beach at the other end of the lake. We'll tie it up there and have lunch; how's that sound?"

"Great."

After lunch, Frank took Brian on a quick tour of the area. He explained, "We're heading up to the summit of the Steens Mountain. From there you can see for hundreds of miles in all directions. When the rest of the family gets here we'll spend a lot more time up here, but I just wanted to show you some spectacular scenery." He showed Brian Keiger Gorge, a huge canyon that descended rapidly toward the Alvord Desert which, as Frank told the boy, was a full mile below where they stood. They drove a little farther and stopped at a viewpoint on the east rim. From there, Frank pointed out the Strawberry Mountains to the northeast, Idaho to the east and Nevada to the south. "That patch of green way down there is the Alvord Ranch."

In the parking lot at the summit, a strong wind buffeted them from the moment they stepped out of the truck. Brian said, "Gramps, this is almost as bad as the wind at Chickahominy Reservoir. Let's get back and do some fishing."

Frank quickly agreed, "Sounds great to me, Boyo. When we come back I hope the wind allows us to spend more time."

On the drive back to camp Brian noticed quite a few small ground squirrels standing up on the rocks. "What're those things, Gramps?"

"Those are little burrowing creatures that I think can be found all over Eastern Oregon. The locals call them graydiggers. I really don't know their proper name, but if graydigger works for them, it's okay with me."

"Graydiggers, huh. It's kind of funny the way they sit up there and then all of a sudden scurry away."

"If you were a meal for most of all the other critters that live around here, including that red-tailed hawk we saw earlier, you'd be a little skittish too."

They bumped along on the road back to camp without any more conversation. Brian watched for graydiggers but looked forward to fishing.

Chapter Twenty-Two

Frank pulled the boat through the water easily. His back toward the bow, he watched as Brian sat in the stern trolling for trout. Brian let out more line, waiting for his first fish. As he rowed the boat out toward the middle of Fish Lake, Frank started to make slow, gradual turns. He explained, "Trolling like this can be very effective here, especially if the person rowing makes some slight changes every once in a while. S-turns and changes in speed can sometimes get a fish to strike the lure. If I remember correctly, we're heading toward a good, deep hole and it wouldn't surprise me if you caught one soon."

Brian watched his line and the tip of his rod carefully. He only grunted in reply.

Trolling through this area, however, did not produce a hit. Frank rowed the boat in a wide turn around the northern end of the lake and started back about 50 yards or so from the eastern shore. He checked to verify their position. He showed Brian how to line up two points on the shore and by keeping the points in a line, one behind the other, maintain a fairly steady heading. Frank relaxed as he rowed; he remembered how much he enjoyed being here. He noticed that he was pulling a little harder with his right arm and for a while paid closer attention to his stroke. When he felt satisfied that his technique was correct he looked up to see where they were. "Oh, boy, we're in too close to the shore. There is a lot of vegetation here that will snag your lure, Brian. Reel in until I turn around again. Okay?"

"Sure thing, Gramps."

As they started in on their next circuit of the lake, Brian let out his line and waited. Soon he had his first trout in the boat. Holding it up he said, "It's not a real big fish, Gramps, should I release it?"

"No, Boyo, that's a keeper here. They stock this lake with rainbow trout. The stockers average about nine inches but they fry up just fine. Three or four are all we need for a meal. The survival rate of small fish when caught and released isn't very good, so you might as well hit it on the head and put it in that bucket."

Frank kept the boat along the western shore, changing speeds and occasionally executing an S-turn by pulling harder with one arm, then switching to the other. It was on one of these turns that he looked up and saw a few runners come over the hill on the southern side of the campground. He was about to point them out to Brian when more runners appeared. "Brian, look up there," he said, "those tents at the far end of the lake must be for those runners."

Brian looked up in time to see yet more runners crest the hill. Dressed in colorful clothing, they headed toward the campground. "Wow! There must be 40 kids."

"There's a sight I wouldn't have expected. I wonder why they're here. Maybe you could walk over there after dinner, Brian, and say hello. They look more or less your age. Hey! This trip may be more fun than you thought it would be, huh?"

Any answer Brian might have had was cut short because at that precise moment a trout struck his line. "Fish on, Gramps; I've got another one."

"That's great, Boyo, that's great."

This trout turned out to be almost identical in size to the first one. "See, Brian, it's another stocker. Add it to the bucket and keep fishing. If we catch a bigger one, maybe a trout from a prior year's stocking, and if we can bring it up to the boat easily, we may release it. It'll depend on how it's hooked."

"Why release the bigger one?"

"Well, if it doesn't swallow the hook and we bring it in quickly then the chances of a big one surviving go way up. And why not let someone else have an opportunity to catch a nice fish. Right?"

"Right; makes sense."

But 20 minutes of fishing produced no more fish.

Brian reeled in and looked back at his grandfather. Frank wondered why. He asked, "Are you tired of fishin' already, Boyo?"

Brian answered with a suggestion, "Hey Gramps, why don't you fish and let me try rowing. Okay?"

"Have you ever rowed a boat before, Brian?"

"No, but how hard can it be? You've been doing all the work; now's my turn."

"Okay, but we have to be very careful trading places. I don't feel like going for a swim just yet."

Frank selected a lure to tie to his set-up and watched as Brian settled into rowing. 'The boy is holding the oars correctly. His stroke seems a little short and he's using too much arm. Should I try correcting him,' he asked himself, 'or should I wait and see if he makes the proper adjustments? I'll let Brian learn this one on his own. This could be an interesting experience for both of us,' Frank thought as he let his line out. For the moment, he concentrated on fishing. He kept an eye on the tip of his rod and the fishing line as it trailed behind the boat.

Brian gripped the oars. He felt the wood beneath his hands. His feet were wedged against the bottom of the seat from which his grandfather fished. Pulling back on the oars he reveled in the immediate feeling of motion, motion he was causing! He turned his head to check where they were in relation to the shore. Satisfied, Brian pushed down with his hands to raise the oars out of the water and leaned forward, pushing as he did so with his arms to position the oars in readiness for the next stroke. He let the oars splash back into the water. At once, his hands felt pressure from the oars so he pulled, starting the next stroke; again they moved forward. He looked up to see Frank smiling back at him.

"Hey Gramps, this is fun."

"It can be, Boyo. Nice and easy ... nice and smooth."

"Yeah, sure; no problem."

Brian was on his fifth stroke when Frank laughed. "Fish on! I've got a fish. Fish on!" He smiled at Brian as he reeled in their third fish. "Now we have all the trout we'll need for dinner tonight, Boyo. Stop rowing while I get this in the bucket and change my set-up to one with a barbless hook. Good job; well done. How do you like rowing so far?"

Brian rested the handles of the oars in his lap. He leaned over them to watch his grandfather change the lure. "I like it! It's kinda fun."

"Great. You're doing just great." Frank nodded toward the southwestern end of the lake and continued, "When we turn around, try to find a nice smooth rhythm, a nice smooth stroke. Okay?"

Following his grandfather's lead, Brian looked over his shoulder and was surprised to see how close they were to shore. They had continued to drift and were now merely 20 feet away. Aquatic vegetation grew here and surrounded them. He thought that if he pulled with one arm and pushed with the other he could turn around, but in doing so they ended up even closer to the shore, the oars tangled in the weeds. Brian tried rowing backwards but simply made matters worse. Now he was getting angry with the weeds and with the boat that wouldn't go where he wanted it to. Then the boat struck a submerged log. They were stuck. Only six feet from the shore, they were hung up on a log. Brian wanted to scream. He threw the oars down in disgust. "Stupid boat! I can't do this!"

Frank watched his grandson carefully. He remembered doing something similar once himself and understood the boy's frustration. He'd been silent until Brian's outburst. 'Now, I gotta stop him before he really gets going.'

"Wait one minute, Boyo. I want you to stop telling lies!" Frank waited for his words to sink in. When he saw Brian stop to look at him he continued, "The statement of 'I can't' is nothing but a big fat lie. You may not have acquired the skills needed to successfully row a boat yet, but that is a far cry from being unable to do so. Now, I want you to listen very carefully to what I'm going to share with you. The human brain is a wonderful and complex instrument. To call it a powerful computer is insulting to your brain. But, to help me make my point, let's call it a super computer. Do you know who programs your brain? Either you do so purposely, or the world will. When you tell yourself you can't, your brain believes it, even if it's not true. It's not the truth. You are lying to yourself. People have died because they believed they could not swim when they fell in the water. The self-instruction and fear associated with the lie 'I can't swim' causes people to tense up, panic and drown simply because they believed the lie. So, you gotta be really careful what you tell yourself; strive for accuracy and avoid exaggeration. This will help you ... give you time to think, to gain perspective ... to understand."

Brian sat still; he tried to relax.

"Hey, I remember a blessing that fits. 'May you always know the truth and honor it, and may you never believe a lie, especially the lies you tell yourself.' "

Frank paused, "Look, I don't know that much about rowing a boat. I'm sure there are skills and techniques that one could learn and practice to become an expert at it. I've gotten good enough over the years to feel comfortable rowing this small boat on a calm lake. I never considered spending more time and effort to really get good at it because, well, it just wasn't that important to me."

"However, you have not even gone through the first steps of learning. The first step of learning is explanation; I really didn't explain what I was doing. The second step is demonstration and I certainly did not demonstrate for you proper rowing skills. I rowed the boat and you watched; they are not the same thing. The third step is imitation, and while you tried to imitate what I was doing, without the first two steps you were bound to have some difficulty. After you learn the skills properly and practice them, repetition is the fourth step. Only then may you achieve mastery. Hey, that reminds me of something one of my coaches used to say all the time. You know that saying 'practice makes perfect'? "

Brian nodded his head yes in reply.

"Well, he would say that's a lie too; the only thing practice makes is permanent. Practice reinforces a habit. A habit is something you've programmed into your brain. No, he would say, only 'perfect practice' makes perfect. If you practice the right skills in the right way, then you are on the path to mastery."

Brian remembered an earlier conversation with his grandfather, smiled and asked slyly, "Then what comes after mastery, Gramps?"

Frank laughed loudly and answered, "That is still something you have to learn for yourself, Boyo, but that was a good try."

Brian thought about what his grandfather said. "But Gramps, we're still stuck on a log and I don't know what to do."

"First off, take a few good deep breaths; exhale like you're trying to fog a mirror. Get all the air out of your lungs. Fill your lungs with good fresh air. This will help you relax. It will send oxygen to your brain and to your muscles. I believe that we learn better when we are relaxed and this deep breathing exercise is a great way to start the relaxation response."

Brian did as he was told. Frank continued, "Okay, pull one of the oars out of the oarlock. That's right, now use the oar to push down and move us away from the log."

When Brian pushed down on the oar the small boat lifted off the log and they glided away.

"Good, now pole us out of these weeds toward the middle of the lake. When we get into deeper water you can start rowing again."

In the middle of the lake Frank asked Brian if he would like to learn how to row the boat better.

"Sure, Gramps that sounds fine."

They switched places carefully. Frank spent a few minutes explaining what he knew of rowing. He held the oars correctly and demonstrated not only a proper stroke, but talked about maneuvering the boat as well.

When he was done Brian tried again and this time did much better. Frank was pleased. "Excellent, Boyo, now why don't we beach this thing, get dinner ready and eat, then after dinner you can check out those runners. You'll have plenty of time this week to practice rowing."

"Okay, Gramps … sounds like a plan."

Brian had seemed eager to meet the runners, so when they were done eating, Frank shooed him away. 'The time will fly by if he has someone besides an old man like me to hang out with.'

Frank's gaze stopped at the fire pit and he realized they had very little firewood. 'I better go for a walk and scrounge up some wood.' He enjoyed a campfire and looked forward to sitting around one with his grandson.

The trail wound down and away from camp. Frank expected to easily find wood, but as he walked, it became obvious that suitable wood was scarce. He'd been walking west, following a small game trail through the aspen, picking up an occasional branch but not finding much at all. He crossed a small clearing and entered the trees on the far side. Already annoyed that he hadn't brought more wood along, Frank became angry when he saw that someone had ripped a live branch off a tree. 'That's just dumb; this entire grove of aspen is one big organism. Green wood doesn't burn well anyway. Why don't people get it? We're here to enjoy nature, not spoil it.'

Frank realized he was feeling upset, so he decided to rest a while. He found a flat rock, sat and took a few deep breaths, exhaling slowly. He concentrated on his breathing and closed his eyes. The sounds of the woods, the birds and the insects became noticeable. He began to feel calm. 'It's not like it's a matter of life and death, it's just firewood. I'll get what I can for tonight and tomorrow we'll just have to go find more.'

While he sat there, letting the woods work its magic, Frank thought about his life —the happy years with Moira when the kids were young, as well as later when things started to unravel. He'd enjoyed this trip so far and eagerly anticipated the time when Robert would arrive with the rest of the family. He felt grateful. The phrase 'the time of your life' came to mind and he said out loud, "Well, I am having the time of my life." He smiled with the realization that all his best memories were times spent with friends and family. 'Life is so precious,' he thought, 'and time so fleeting. We really should make the most of what we have.' The thought occurred to him that he would like to see Meg again. He got up and continued looking for wood.

After returning, Frank looked at the small pile of firewood. 'At least we have enough wood for a decent campfire with a little left over,' thought Frank, 'enough for an hour or so; I just won't start it until Brian returns. In the meantime, I'll think I'll sit in the camper and read.' He studied the available books in the cupboard before pulling down a well used copy of 'Seven Habits.' 'There's something I want to check in here,' he mused, 'that's right, here it is ... begin with the end in mind ... mmm, to begin with the end in mind means to start with a clear understanding of your destination. I need to talk to Brian about how that relates to learning a new skill.'

Frank spent some time reading before closing his book. He stepped out of the camper and took a deep breath. The breeze was back and the trees shimmered in the twilight. The stars were only now starting to pop out, and in the west a soft salmon-colored sunset brightened the horizon. 'What a nice evening; I'm so glad to be here.' He settled into one of the camp chairs near the fire pit, rested his legs on the largest rock and closed his eyes.

The sound of laughter roused Frank from his nap. He looked around. The sky was much darker now, the sunset gone, many more stars could be seen; pinpricks of light strewn everywhere. He heard Brian's voice, "It's right here somewhere; I wish we had a flashlight."

Frank chuckled and called out. "Hey Brian, over here."

Brian stepped into the campsite, "Hey Gramps, I've got company." He was accompanied by three other young people. "These are my friends." He started with the tall boy on the end, "This is Neil, this is Vanessa, and Jacob; they are part of a running camp. They're here doing high-altitude training. Guys, this is my Gramps, Frank Kilgore."

"Hi Mr. Kilgore; I'm Neil Mezzasalma; nice to meet you." Neil extended his hand as he stepped forward.

Frank reached for and shook Neil's hand and answered with, "It's a pleasure to meet you Neil. Please, call me Frank."

"Okay, Frank."

A young girl of medium height stepped forward. "And my name is Vanessa Evans."

The third youth stepped forward to shake hands. He was of medium height and build with light hair that hung down almost to his shoulders. "Hi Frank, I'm Jacob, er, Jacob Minter."

In the darkness it was hard for Frank to see the newcomers clearly, but he could see that Neil was tall, perhaps six foot, six or seven inches, and thin. He had dark hair and angular features.

Vanessa had a pleasant smile and curly, almost frizzy hair. "Well then, let me get this campfire started so we can see a little better."

Frank lit a match and used it to ignite the tinder and kindling he'd prepared under the stack of wood. Soon, the fire blazed into life scattering its light to the area.

"Gramps, the kids over at the running camp are having a bonfire and a marshmallow roast. We were wondering, do you have any marshmallows along?"

"Of course. I never go camping without all the ingredients for s'mores. In fact, I even have extra graham crackers and chocolate bars, if you're interested."

"Sweet. Can we take 'em, Gramps?"

"WHY SOITENLY!"

Vanessa laughed and spoke up, "Oh, thank you Mr. Kilgore; that's so nice of you."

"Not at all Vanessa, and please, call me Frank."

"Okay Frank, thanks, s'mores sound great."

Frank thought for a minute about where he had packed the marshmallows and graham crackers; he knew the chocolate bars were in the camper. "Brian, please come with me to the camper. I'll get you a flashlight and the candy bars and then you can dig out a bag of marshmallows and a box of graham crackers from the big plastic tub on the table over there, okay?"

"Sure thing, Gramps ... thanks."

When Frank returned to the campfire the flames danced brightly. The fire snapped and crackled. Frank could now see that although Neil was thin he had a strong, wiry build. When he smiled, Neil's face seemed to light up. Vanessa carried herself with poise and confidence. Jacob's face was dominated by a large nose and prominent cheekbones. All looked fit and were obviously athletes.

Brian searched the container with the flashlight for the graham crackers and marshmallows. He found them and rejoined the group at the campfire. "Here's all the stuff. Hey Neil, could you grab this from me?" Brian asked, indicating the bag of marshmallows.

"Sure thing."

"I'll carry the chocolate bars," Vanessa volunteered.

"Okay, well, let's get going. Thanks, Gramps."

"Have fun, Boyo; have fun. I think I'll sit around the fire awhile. Maybe if you're not too late gettin' back, we can talk."

Brian answered with hesitation, "Yeah, sure, but I don't know when I'll be back, Gramps."

"Whenever's fine Brian; don't worry about it."

Neil added, "It won't be too late, Brian. We're really tired after the long run we had today; I'll bet some kids are already in bed. I know I'm pretty tired."

"Me too," Vanessa chimed in.

"Okay then, you kids run along and have fun. Whenever you get back is fine. Don't forget to take the flashlight with you. Go, have fun."

"Thanks Gramps, you're too cool."

Brian and his new friends shared good-natured banter as they walked away from where Frank sat. The sound of youthful laughter brought a smile to his face. He said to the night, "Ah, to be young again."

Frank watched the stars for a while and enjoyed the fire. He decided to let it burn down, thinking that when Brian returned he might add the rest of the wood if the boy wanted to stay up awhile. But later, when Brian did come back, he felt tired and wanted to go to bed. Frank doused the red glowing embers with water. He stirred it, added more water and when he was satisfied that it was completely out, joined Brian, who had already gone to the camper.

Chapter Twenty-Three

From the darkness surrounding him, Frank figured it must be well before dawn. He rolled over in his sleeping bag to lie on his back. Closing his eyes, he settled back into bed. He heard a low rumble in the distance and listened carefully. A short while later he heard it again. This time it seemed louder as well as closer. 'That's thunder,' he thought. A louder rumble, this one nearer yet, confirmed his guess. Frank quickly thought about their gear and the campsite. 'Everything is stowed away; the boat is beached so it's okay. The tent and gazebo are staked down so they're fine. The tarp! The tarp covering the stuff on the table is not secure. If the wind takes the tarp and it rains hard all that gear will get wet. I better get up and secure it before it starts raining.'

He swung his legs over the edge of the bed when a louder crash, followed by a flash of lightning, persuaded him to hurry. Dressing quickly, he had just finished tying his shoes when another loud crash echoed through the mountains.

"Gramps, what's that?" asked Brian in a sleepy voice.

"It sounds like we're in for a storm, Brian. That's thunder. I'm going out to tie down the tarp on the table before it starts raining."

Frank flipped on the camper's porch light. He opened the door and stepped out into the early morning. Closing the door of the camper behind him, Frank stood briefly on the steps to get his bearings. From the valley, thunder crashed again, followed seconds later by lightning. It provided Frank with all the light he needed to orient himself. Quickly, he walked to the table. He could smell rain in the air. He reached under the tarp, where he remembered a small plastic container held bungee cords. 'Good, there it is; let's get this done in a hurry. It's just a matter of time before it rains.'

When he was satisfied the tarp was secured he hurried back to the camper. He'd just opened the door when a bright flash of lightning split the darkness. It startled him; he jumped. Standing at the top of the steps he counted, one Mississippi, two Mississippi, three Mississippi, four … a loud, rolling crack of thunder exploded. He heard Brian exclaim, "Wow! That was close!"

"It sure was, Boyo, it sure was."

Thunder crashed loudly all around them. Peals of thunder followed the lightning more and more closely until they seemed to be a single event. Then it started to rain.

At first, the rain on the roof sounded like small pebbles striking the top of a garbage can. Later, it became a constant roar punctuated by deafening crashes of thunder. The camper shook.

Brian had sat up for a while looking out the window when the storm struck. He was amazed at how loud the thunder sounded and at first felt compelled to watch the lightning as it lit up the sky. As time went on and the storm showed no signs of diminishing, he lay back down and pulled his sleeping bag close around him.

Right about daybreak, Frank decided to stow his bedding and set up the table. For a short time he just sat listening to the storm. After a particularly loud clap of thunder, he heard Brian say, "Is this going to go on all day, or what?"

Frank answered with something he often said, "The weather is going to do what the weather is going to do. There's no sense complaining about it … or worrying about it … since there is nothing we can DO about it; right?"

"I guess."

"Well, Boyo, you might as well get up. Let's have some breakfast and afterwards we can read or play cards until the storm blows over."

Breakfast was simple, cereal with juice and dried fruit. The dishes were cleaned and put away. The storm still raged outside.

The rain beat constantly against the roof of the camper. The thunder and lightning let up. Brian looked up at the small collection of books and decided to take a closer look at his grandfather's 'Bulletin Board.' He pulled it down from the shelf and removed the rubber band. "When did you start this, Gramps?" he asked as he held it up.

"That thing ... let me see, I guess about 20 or so years ago. I noticed that whenever I came across an article or story that I liked I would add it to my collection. I soon realized that in many cases I could organize them into topics, so I bought this diary, but I didn't want to keep a traditional diary, so I named it 'My Bulletin Board.' "

"You know, Gramps, you can do the same thing on a computer just by creating folders and files."

"I know that Brian; in fact, I have done exactly that on my computer at home, but I still like to have this handy. In fact, I still add newspaper articles and other printed stuff to it from time to time. I like looking through it once in a while. If you're going to read that, would you reach up and hand me the 'Seven Habits of Highly Effective People?' There's something I want to check on."

"Oh, okay."

Brian skimmed through the Bulletin Board. There didn't seem to be any particular order to things and he became interested in his grandfather's humor section first. He laughed at many of the cartoons and jokes that he found. Occasionally, he would find a really funny cartoon and show it to Frank. Most of the time, his grandfather would look at the cartoon or joke and chuckle. Once, when Brian held up a 'Far Side' cartoon Frank laughed loudly and said, "I remember that one. That's funny, isn't it?"

"Yeah, it is."

In the back of the book, Brian found a few index cards. The titles read 'Re-Affirmation Number One' and so on. He read a few of these and felt compelled to ask his grandfather about them. "What're these, Gramps?"

Frank reached across the table and took the index cards from Brian. He thumbed through them. He smiled at one and held it up. "Well, Boyo," he started, "Remember yesterday when I said that the human brain is like a super computer?"

"Yeah."

"These are self-instructions. On one of my jobs, I received some sales training and this technique was part of that training. You see, if you continually repeat a re-affirmation or self-instruction with enough conviction, enough times, you program yourself to believe it. I used this one when I found myself gaining too much weight." He slid the index card across the table for Brian to read.

Brian picked it up and read out loud, " 'I control my overeating. I ONLY eat reasonable portions of healthy, nutritious foods. I drink plenty of clear, healthy water every day and take vitamins to support my health. I ALWAYS exercise at least three times a week. I feel more energy and vitality every day. My body is very efficient. I will live a long and healthy life filled with love, humility and contribution. These habits support me. These habits enable me to provide a good model for my loved ones and my friends.' " Brian looked up from the card and asked, "Does this stuff really work?"

"I believe so. I think when you frame the self-instruction correctly you're picking how you want to be. So, you choose your attitude. Then by stating the behaviors you want, you build a new set of habits. The re-affirmation reinforces whatever 'habit' you've decided to adopt. Through repetition it actually becomes real for you. Have you ever heard the saying 'you can achieve anything if you believe that you can'? "

"Yeah, my dad says that all the time."

"Well, it's true; the way we look at things, the way we process information, the way we react to certain situations, all these things are based upon our habits. If you learn to control the way you think and the way you build your own habits, then eventually you can achieve whatever you set your mind to."

"What do you mean, control the way you think?"

"Okay, look, this is easier than it sounds ... let's see ... what's a good example? Let's say you grew up in a really strict house and that whenever you did something wrong, one of your parents punished you severely. As you got older, whenever you felt that maybe you were doing something wrong you would have an emotional experience just like when you were a little kid. This gut reaction might lead you to become confrontational or avoid the situation that caused it. This is called the fight or flight reaction. Anyway in many instances your gut reaction is wrong. If you could step back for a while and think things through, you would, most likely, arrive at a better solution. Here's another one of my self-instructions." Frank picked up another index card and read, "I ALWAYS approach every situation in a calm and wise manner. Wisdom is being able to weigh all the elements in a cool and detached way, judge the best alternative or response and do what is JUST and what is BEST for all involved."

"You mean that if I repeat something like this enough times that when something happens to me I'll react the way I want to?"

"Exactly; remember the super computer? Your brain wants to be programmed; it needs to be programmed. Far better for you to program your own brain, than to let other forces program it for you. All this stuff," Frank said with a wave of his hand toward the Bulletin Board, "has something to do about the way we think or how we build our habits. If I found a movie or a book or even a song that had a message or a lesson that I liked ... that had some meaning for me, I included it in my journal. The lessons in here are things I want in here; they're my pearls of wisdom."

"Pearls of wisdom?"

"Yes, pearls of wisdom; do you remember when I said lessons come to us from many different places?"

"Yeah."

"Well, what if in every story you hear or read … every movie you see or song you hear there is at least one really good lesson? It may be hidden inside the story, or it may be the main point of the story, but in either case it's there for you IF you find it. If you are ready for that particular lesson, well then, there's a precious 'gem of truth' or 'pearl of wisdom' for you to use. Get it?"

"I guess," replied Brian with some hesitation.

"Look, here's an example," Frank said pointing up toward the small collection of books in the cabinet, "there are lessons in each of these books if you want to find them. Each book has a message or lesson that you could benefit from. Isaac Asimov wrote a number of books about robots that were the basis for the movie *Bicentennial Man*, which is a movie about a robot, but it's really about human potential. *A Christmas Carol* isn't just a cute ghost story. It is a blueprint for anyone who really wants to examine their life and change. Anyone can review events in their life from the past, compare those events with what's happening in their life now and guess what'll happen if things don't change. The key is … always be looking for the little pearl of wisdom; you'll be surprised how many are out there."

"How do you know a pearl of wisdom when you see one?"

"That is a great question. You don't always know at the time. We may see a lesson many times before it actually has meaning for us, or we may need an answer and—" Frank snapped his fingers for emphasis, "—suddenly there it is. But if you don't look for it in the first place you'll never find it. Ask and it shall be yours; seek and you shall find."

Brian read again the first re-affirmation and thought about what his grandfather had said. He started to read more of the index cards when he was surprised to hear a knock on the door.

Sitting near the door, Frank was startled by the knock as well. He stood up, turned and opened the door. He recognized two of the runners Brian had brought over last night. "What a pleasant surprise," he said, "Neil and Vanessa."

"Hi Mr. Kilgore. I got tired of sitting in my tent and, well, we thought we'd come over to say hi."

"Just call me Frank, Neil, and please come on in."

"Okay, Frank … thanks. After you, Vanessa," Neil said as he stepped back to let her by. Brian slid the index cards back into the Bulletin Board before closing it. He placed it on the side of the table and greeted his friends, "Hey there, Vanessa … Neil, some storm huh?"

Neil replied, "You can say that again."

"Hi Brian. Hi Frank," Vanessa said. Once she was in the camper she added, "I brought you some trail mix since you were so kind to let us have the marshmallows and stuff last night."

"Oh, you didn't need to do that," replied Frank.

"I wanted to. Besides, my mom sent enough trail mix with me to last two weeks, not one."

"Well, that's very nice of you; thank you." Frank accepted the trail mix. He reached up into the small cabinet above the sink and pulled out a plastic bowl. "We might as well have a snack as long as we have company, right, Brian?" Frank poured the trail mix into the bowl before placing it on the table.

He moved farther back to give Vanessa a clear path to the table. Brian slid to his left to give her room.

Instead of sitting down at the table, Neil stood in the doorway and looked around before he smiled and said, "After being stuck in a leaky tent all morning it sure feels good to be able to stand up straight. Frank, do you want to sit here?" indicating the seat at the table.

"Sure Neil, let's trade places."

"Your tent leaked?" Brian asked as Neil moved over to stand in front of the stove.

"Yeah, it leaked but not too bad; just enough to make things a little uncomfortable." Neil looked over at Vanessa and laughed before adding, "It was nowhere near as bad as Jacob's tent." Neil shook his head and still laughing, continued, "His tent leaked and ... they set it up in a low area. They woke up with their air mattress floating in the middle of a puddle."

Vanessa added with a chuckle, "Jacob said that after it thundered for awhile he fell back to sleep and when he woke up his hand was in a puddle. He said he looked around, saw all the water, and just rolled over and tried to go back to sleep."

Brian said, "Good luck with that, huh?"

"Yeah," she replied, "Everything in his tent is just soaked. We couldn't go for the morning run, what with the lightning and all. So, when Neil suggested visiting you guys, I thought ... why not."

"We're happy to have the company," Frank said. "We've just been reading."

"This is a lot more comfortable then my tent. Plus, I can stand up straight," Neil said while stretching. "Ah! That feels good."

"Hey, Neil, I forgot to tell my grandfather about your uncle's restaurant. Gramps, Neil is a busboy in his uncle's restaurant."

"Yeah, that's right, Brian told us about what you guys did in Burns. That's really cool. We were shorthanded a couple of months ago. I never worked so hard in my life."

"Tell us about your uncle's place Neil; what kind of a restaurant is it?"

"It's not a real fancy place but it's fairly popular. We specialize in Italian food. It's called 'Nona Concetta's' after my great-grandmother. We serve pretty authentic Italian food. All my cousins work there too. I'm mostly a busboy but I do wait tables once in a while."

"How do you like it?"

"It's cool. I work mostly with family; my cousins are fun and my uncle is, well, he's a nut sometimes but he's cool to work for."

"What do you like best?"

"Well, when I get a chance to wait tables I like dealing with the customers. Recently my uncle has been teaching me how to make espresso drinks; that's cool too."

"Ah, I love a good latté. Can you do the art with the foam?"

"Not so well yet, but my uncle is amazing. He can do like leaves and hearts and like, other stuff too."

"I guess getting good at doing the art well takes practice, huh?"

"You bet. But my uncle says that it's more important to get the foam right than to be able to do the art. When the foam is right the drink will taste good. He says having nice art on a latté shows the customer that you made the drink especially for them and that it's done correctly."

"Your uncle sounds like pleasing the customer is important to him. What else does he say?"

"He believes that there are some really important moments to give the customer good service." Neil paused before continuing, "Greet the customer in a friendly way. Make them feel welcome."

Frank nodded his head and said simply, "Yes."

"Make sure you refill their glasses before they empty their glass, but always ask before you refill their coffee. He says bringing the next course at the right time is really important too."

"Very good. Is there more?"

"Well, bringing the desserts and presenting the check; oh, and he always goes on about having good bread and coffee. He hates going to a restaurant and having a good meal but not good bread or coffee."

Frank nodded his head in agreement, "Me too; I hate that. What else does he say?"

Neil smiled before continuing, "He's always going on about rotating all the food properly. I've only seen him really mad once. He found a container of cheese that was outdated and went bad; he really went off. He kept asking everyone if they were blind or something or didn't they care that our stuff went bad."

"I remember my old boss doing the same thing. Rotating the food properly is really important, not only for the customers but for your employer as well."

Neil nodded in agreement and then remembered something else, "Oh, and my uncle better not catch you standing in front of the refrigerator with the door open."

Frank interrupted with a laugh, "The only time I ever remember my old boss, Tony, yelling was when someone kept the door of the refrigerator open; he'd yell, CLOSE THE REFRIGERATOR!"

"My uncle does the same thing."

"When you think about it, knowing what you are going into the refrigerator for, opening it quickly, getting the food and closing the door right away helps keep the food in the refrigerator fresh and it also saves the boss on energy costs."

"And," Neil added, "my uncle would also say it doesn't hurt the life of the equipment either."

"That's true too, Neil."

Frank smiled at Neil and turning toward Brian asked, "When you were working with Meg did she teach you anything we haven't talked about?"

"I don't know. I spent most of the time clearing and setting tables. There was one thing though; she saved one of the tables in the back of the restaurant for a couple of regular customers. She told me the guy was a little hard of hearing and that background noise bothered him. Seating them in the back helped with that, so she always tried to seat there."

Vanessa, who had been quietly listening to the conversation now smiled mischievously and said, "Huh?"

Brian looked at her in puzzlement and repeated, "He was a little hard of hearing so they liked to sit at a table in the back."

"Huh?"

"He was hard of hearing so … Oh! Very funny."

They all laughed at Vanessa's practical joke and at Brian's response. Always ready to appreciate someone with a good sense of humor, Frank looked at Vanessa more closely. She had a twinkle in her eye and a happy smile.

Brian looked up at Neil and asked, "So, it sounds like you like it there?"

"Yeah, it's okay, and I am getting better at it. It's kinda cool working with my cousins too."

Vanessa reached over to the Bulletin Board. She pulled it toward her and asked, "What's this?"

Brian explained, "That's my grandfather's journal. He calls it his Bulletin Board. It's got a lot of stuff in it about different things; I was reading it when you guys came."

Vanessa asked Frank if she could look through it.

"Be my guest my dear; have at it."

Brian changed the subject and started a conversation with Neil about running. As the two boys talked, Vanessa silently thumbed through the pages. "Oh, I like this," she muttered softly.

"What's that, Vanessa?" Frank asked. The boys fell silent.

She looked up somewhat startled but recovered quickly. "You have this whole section on habits, about learning good habits and checking to see if the habits you already have help you, and that's all cool but this one is really good." She read from the book, " 'Habits can be changed without changing the person. So, it's not about trying to change the person, it's about adjusting a habit or a set of skills.' " She paused and looked up at Frank. "My coach says something like that. She says that we should develop habits that work for us and weed out those that don't. Last month she showed me that I had developed a little, er, hitch in my stride. We worked on it for weeks before I straightened it out. My stride is way smoother now."

Frank answered with a grin, "Sounds like you have a good coach, Vanessa."

"Yeah, she's great. You know what else she says about bad habits?"

"What?"

"A bad habit is six times harder to change once it becomes a habit than if you learned to do it right in the first place."

"I believe it."

Chapter Twenty-four

"Frank, I don't get this." Vanessa had been reading the Bulletin Board while the boys chatted on. "What's it about?"

Frank had been listening to the boys as they talked and to the storm outside. Vanessa's question startled him. His head jerked up and he stammered, "Huh? Excuse me?"

Vanessa held up a half sheet of paper. "This quote here: 'Intellectual understanding is a threshold process, necessary for learning, but not sufficient for lasting improvement. Deep change requires the retooling of ingrained habits of thought, feeling and behavior.' It's by Daniel Goleman from *Working with Emotional Intelligence*."

The boys became silent and looked to Frank for his answer. "Okay, Vanessa please repeat the quote. I'd like to make sure I frame my answer correctly."

Vanessa read the quote again before passing the paper across the table to Frank. He turned it around with his fingers, and began, "Let me use the way we learn a new skill as an example. When you are first taught a new skill, you should have the skill explained to you before you're shown how to do it. You should understand what's involved. If that's clear then you can move on to the next step, which would be the student trying the skill. At this stage, your coach might watch you to make sure you're doing it right. In any case, now you can practice the skill and make it a habit."

"Kinda like what we were talking about before?"

"Sort of. What I think he's saying here is ... in order to really change a deep-seated attitude, a way of looking at things or even a set of habits ... you must re-create and change ... not only the way you think about it, but also the way you feel about it, in order to change the way you act. You have to shift from one perspective to another."

"Why?" asked Brian, "I don't get it."

To all the teens Frank answered, "Okay, let me explain it differently. Brian and I have been talking about how the clear use of words affects how well we communicate. When you ask a question clearly, you actually help the person who has to answer it. It makes the whole process better. For two people to communicate well they should at least acknowledge the other's point of view. The idea of perspective is valuable to think about here. Do you all know what perspective means exactly?"

Neil answered tentatively, "Isn't it, um, how you interpret something based on your history?"

"Yes, it's someone's unique point of view. The better we know the other person's point of view the better our communication will be. By the way, the better your communication is, the easier it will be for you to get along with other people. Therefore, good clear communication helps you live well. Anyway, where was I? Oh yes ... would you agree that taking the other person's point of view into consideration helps us to understand better?"

Neil and Brian both nodded their heads. Vanessa asked, "Okay, but how does this apply to 'deep change and retooling ingrained habits?'"

"Good question, Vanessa; I was just getting to that. Suppose a person develops a bad habit in the way they communicate. Say they start to come up with an answer before the other person is finished. In other words, they sort of assume they know what the other person is going to say and then they prepare an answer without really listening to the whole thing. Let us also say that because they do this they're in the habit of interrupting people."

"I hate when that happens," Neil added, "I have a friend that does it all the time."

"I think we all know someone who does this and sometimes we're all a bit guilty of doing it, too. In any case, to replace the interrupting behavior with something better, a person has to change the very way they think. A better alternative is to develop a habit of really trying to understand before responding. To change the old habit, one has to think differently about how they listen, and feel differently about the other person before they can change their behavior."

Vanessa looked puzzled. "What do you mean by 'feel differently' about the other person?"

"Wouldn't you agree that trying to understand someone is respectful of them? Interrupting is not respectful. I guess I'm talking about empathy; the ability to put yourself in the other person's shoes, so to speak."

"Yeah, I get it," answered Vanessa.

"Hey, it's like one of your jokes, Gramps," Brian chuckled, 'Never criticize someone till you've walked a mile in their shoes. That way, you're a mile away and you have their shoes.' "

When the laughter subsided, Neil cleared his throat. "It's getting close to lunchtime so we need to get back. And it looks like the rain is letting up."

Brian looked out the window and agreed, "Yeah, and the sun is coming out too."

"I'm really glad we came over; at least I got to stand up for a while."

"I was going to invite you kids to stay for lunch," Frank said, "Do you have to go back?"

Neil answered, "Yeah, they want us to all eat together. The food isn't too bad."

Vanessa added, "But I do miss my mom's cooking."

"Do you have any free time after lunch?" Frank asked the question as if he had something in mind.

"Well, yes. Our afternoon training doesn't start till two. Why?

"We have a pie that was given to us at the restaurant. We'd be happy to share some with you kids. It's hazelnut and supposedly one of Bert's specialties."

Vanessa looked interested and asked, "Is it like pecan?"

"Yep."

"That sounds great. What do you think, Neil?"

"Sounds good to me too. Count us in."

Frank replied, "Then we'll see you back here after lunch."

After Neil and Vanessa left, Brian, lacking anything better to do, sat reading more of the Bulletin Board as his grandfather quickly prepared a small lunch. "You know, Gramps there is a lot of cool stuff in here."

"I'm glad you think so, Brian. Is there anything in particular that you like?"

"There's a poem here in the back that's kinda interesting. It's called 'Perpetual Caterpillars'. "

"Oh, I'm glad you brought that one up. I wanted to show it to you anyway. Why don't you read it out loud?"

"Okay," replied Brian. He read, " 'Woe to those poor caterpillars … confined to myopic meandering …whose limited vision … condemns them … to perpetual wandering. When all that is needed is … surrender … to the cocoon … to the shelter of the self. Emerging resplendent … able to fly … to see … to soar! A caterpillar no more'. "

"Do you like that?"

"Sort of, but I'm not sure I know what it means."

"Why don't you think about it for a minute while I get our meal ready and we'll discuss it during lunch. Okay?"

"Sure thing, Gramps."

Frank soon had the lunch prepared and on the table. Brian sat reading the poem again as he chewed on his food. "What does 'myopic' mean, Gramps?"

"Shortsighted."

"Oh."

"So Brian, what do you think it means?"

"Um, well, since a caterpillar can't see very far it really doesn't see much; it just crawls around. Then, when it becomes a butterfly, well, it can fly and see much more. But what does it mean ... the shelter of the self?"

Frank nodded his head in approval. "You're right. This is something we've been talking about. If you as an individual have a choice about what you think, how you feel, and how you behave, then you and you alone get to decide what kind of person you become. You are responsible for yourself and answerable to yourself. Basically it's saying that if you accept that responsibility you can soar like a butterfly, not crawl around like a caterpillar."

Brian took another bite of his sandwich and read the poem again as he chewed. "Hmmm, okay I guess."

Frank waited while Brian silently reread the poem.

Brian asked, "We have a choice how we feel?"

"Yes, absolutely." Frank reached up to the cabinet and pulled a book from the shelf. "This book, *Man's Search for Meaning*, was written by a man named Viktor Frankl. He wrote it after spending the Second World War as a prisoner in Nazi concentration camps. He survived Auschwitz, one of the worst ones. The point of his book is that the Nazis could imprison him, they could take away his freedom, they could even take away his life but they could not take away his basic personal freedom, his freedom to decide how he chose to respond ... his freedom to choose how he felt. Frankl lost almost his entire family, only he and a sister survived the war, but Victor Frankl chose not to lose his humanity under the most inhumane conditions. He shows us that we always have a choice and that the responsibility for our decisions lies within us all. It is an amazing story with, at its heart, a huge lesson."

"I, uh, I'm not sure I get it, Gramps. How do you do that … decide how you feel?"

"Yeah, it sounds simple but it's not that simple to do. It all starts with awareness. If you become aware of how you feel about something, then you can judge for yourself if that is the way you want to feel about it. If it's not, then you can take steps to change. Without awareness though, without paying attention, there can be no change."

Brian listened carefully to what his Grandfather had said. He spoke with such conviction that Brian wanted to understand. However, it sounded somewhat unreal; it couldn't be that simple. Could it? He wondered, 'If it is this simple, why haven't I heard about it before? Does everyone know about this?' He needed to think some more. To himself, he reread the poem. Then he reached over toward Frankl's book. He picked it up and read the cover before turning it over and reading the back.

"Should I read this, Gramps?"

"I think everyone should, Brian."

"Okay, I'll read it this week."

Frank replied, "Sweet!"

Having decided to read *Man's Search for Meaning*, Brian pushed it to the side and continued to thumb through Frank's Bulletin Board. It seemed to have three main sections even though his grandfather had added many random quotes and writings amongst the pages. He found a section his grandfather had entitled 'The Art of Living Well.' At the top of page one, Frank had written: Basic Rules for Living Well. Under this, he had 10 numbers with the rules themselves.

Brian turned the page to the next section. At the top of this page, in bold print was the word: 'Love.'

Under this heading Frank seemed to have just randomly added titles of books, quotes and song titles. Brian recognized several of the titles. One quote from Ursula Le Guin caught his attention and Brian read, "Love just doesn't sit there like a stone, it has to be made like bread, remade all the time, made new."

A sticky note had a word with which Brian was not familiar. Written in big block letters, the word AGAPE was defined as 'the love one feels for others without any sexual or sensual connotations; it is the love for fellow human beings simply because they are worthy of love.'

Brian read with interest but soon realized that many of the things he'd read were more complex than they seemed to be at first. 'I'm gonna have to study this before I really get it.'

He skimmed through the last section. He was disappointed to find that this section seemed incomplete. In fact, the place on top of the page where Brian would have expected to see a title was blank. The lower half of the page contained a variety of general quotes and thoughts that didn't seem to be related in any way. He was about to ask his grandfather about it when he heard Neil's voice. Brian looked up to see Neil and Vanessa approach the camper. Neil spoke loudly, "Hey, Brian, we're back. I've been thinking about that pie ever since we left."

Frank opened the door and laughed, "Come on in. I've been thinking about it too. Let's see how good it is."

Frank cut into the pie and served up a slice for each of them. Once they had all taken a seat at the table he watched as the teens ate their first bite.

Vanessa said, "Wow, this is delicious!"

Neil swallowed and sighed with pleasure. "This is great!"

Brian ate his first bite and agreed, "Delicious! Gramps, you gotta try it. You're gonna love it!"

"What! Something other then blueberry pie meets your approval?" Frank asked in a teasing way.

"Yes, I do like it." Brian answered, "You're hilarious Gramps, just hilarious."

Frank explained to Neil and Vanessa about Brian's favorite pie and was surprised that Neil also admitted to liking one pie above others. "I love apple pie," he said "with or without ice cream."

Vanessa reacted with surprise, "But don't you try other kinds?"

"Not when there's apple available, but now I might want to try others if they're as good as this."

Frank chewed on his second bite. The toasted flavor of the hazelnuts stood out in contrast to the sweet filling. The flakey, buttery piecrust melted in his mouth. He swallowed and said, "Bert sure does know his pie. This is great! A person would be hard pressed not to enjoy such wonderful pie. It's obviously baked with pride."

"Gramps, is this what you were getting at … about honoring yourself by providing great customer service? Bert can feel honored by doing such a good job and delighting his customers, right?"

"Exactly."

They ate the pie with delight and without further conversation. Once the plates were cleared, Frank suggested they step outside since the weather had cleared.

Vanessa held up the Bulletin Board and asked, "Hey Frank, is it okay if we take this outside?"

"Why?"

"I want to look at it some more."

"Sure."

Frank loved the smell of Eastern Oregon after a summer rain. 'The air smells washed and the rain will keep the dust down for a day or so.' He took the opportunity to check on a few things, especially the items under the tarp. He was pleased to see the tarp had remained secure despite the storm's ferocity. He started to undo the bungee cords. Neil stood near the table. "Neil. Would you mind helping me fold this tarp?"

"Sure, Frank; no problem."

"Thanks, grab the other end ... yep, that's right. Now fold it over ... perfect. Thank you."

When they finished folding the tarp, Frank noticed something odd about the way Neil held himself. He studied the boy for a minute before he realized what it was. Although Neil was very tall, he seemed to slouch at the shoulders. Frank watched him carefully as he walked over to join Brian and Vanessa near the fire pit. Frank confirmed that Neil definitely stood with a slouch. He chose his words carefully, "Neil, has anyone ever told you that your posture could use a little improvement?"

"Yeah," Neil responded sheepishly, "my mom tells me that all the time. I really need to work on it."

When Frank asked Neil about his posture he also guessed Brian might be concerned. His grandson looked worried that perhaps this question might embarrass his new friend. Neil's easy response told Frank that the boy seemed okay with it. "I wonder what benefit you get from slouching."

"Benefit?" Neil looked and sounded puzzled. "There's no benefit from slouching."

"Then why do you do it? There must be some reason or payoff for you or you wouldn't have made it a habit."

"Huh? I don't know what you mean."

"Okay, let me see," Frank said. "I want to ask you a few questions. How tall are you Neil? Six-five...Six-six?"

"Yeah, six-six."

"Hmmm..." Frank turned to Vanessa. "Vanessa would you say Neil here is nice?"

"He sure is." she responded enthusiastically, "I've known Neil since fifth grade. He's one of the nicest guys I know."

Frank nodded thoughtfully before addressing Neil. "I think I know what's going on here. I've seen this before. One of my friends, Kevin, was the tallest kid in our grade and he was really nice too. As Kevin got older, he started to slouch as a way of being deferential. In other words, in order to avoid coming across as intimidating, Kevin would sort of lower himself to match the height of those around him. It was his way of being courteous and fitting in better. However, slouching like that is not good for your health. Good posture opens up your airways and helps you avoid long-term back problems. Does that make sense?"

"Yeah, I guess."

"Okay then, this is just what we talking about before. You have a habit, slouching, that you might want to change but if you do not replace your attitude about why you slouch ... as well as the habit itself ... you probably won't succeed. You need to change not only the behavior, but also how you think and feel about standing tall."

Neil looked interested in what Frank was saying but it was Vanessa that spoke first. "I get it," she said excitedly, "he has to change everything in order to really change. But didn't we say that it's a lot harder to change a bad habit?"

"That's correct. A bad habit like this can be compared to a wild horse. It does what it wants to do. Up till now you've let it. It is essential for you to tame the horse before you can retrain it. The habit, er, the horse doesn't want to be changed; it will fight you every step of the way."

"Then what can Neil do, Gramps?"

"There are a number of things, but the first step is to see the habit for what it is."

Brian remembered something his grandfather said earlier, "Awareness is the first step."

"Exactly."

"Then what?" Brian spoke for all.

"Okay, let's say that Neil agrees he slouches so he won't seem so imposing because of his height. And let us also agree that he understands the short-term and the long-term benefits of good posture. Based on that, he could frame a re-affirmation that would allow him to replace his slouching habit with a standing tall habit."

"Is that hard to do?" Neil looked at Frank doubtfully.

"Well, you'd have to really want to. But, no, it's not too hard."

"What do I do?"

"Well, first let's talk about why you slouch. You don't want to be imposing but you are very tall. You have an imposing figure. You will be an imposing man. That's not to say you can't be gentle or kind. Just the opposite is true. If you carry yourself with kindness and concern for those around you, then you won't be intimidating. If you've ever had any training in a martial art, then you would know the way of the warrior: 'As you go through life, pay attention'." Frank warmed to his task when he saw interest in all the kids' eyes. He continued, "Live life with every breath, live in service to others and live with compassion. That is the way of the warrior. You can decide to travel through life as a peaceful warrior, respectful of those around you. Then they will not be intimidated by your height but rather drawn toward your kindness."

Frank walked over to Vanessa and took the Bulletin Board from her. He pulled out an index card. "You need to think up a re-affirmation like this one that will work for you. For example, you could say something like, I always stand tall. I am proud of myself and the way in which I treat others. Good posture promotes good health and allows me to breathe correctly. I practice the habit of good posture not only for myself but as a positive role model for my friends and loved ones."

Neil brought his finger to his lips and with half-closed eyes nodded his head and smiled. "I like that."

"Good; now you have to write something like that on five index cards. Writing it five times helps reinforce it in your mind. If you only do one, your horse will help you lose it. You see, we still have to deal with your horse; it does not want to change. In fact, your horse will do everything in its power to stop you from changing. This is how you must tame your horse. Read the re-affirmation many times for as long as it takes before it actually becomes a new habit. Read it out loud whenever possible and read it with conviction and feeling. If, ah, you're in a public place you'd probably want to read it to yourself so the guys in the white suits don't come for you with a straitjacket, but you should read it out loud at least at the end of the day as you get ready for sleep. Remember, read it with feeling; read it as if it were already accomplished. These repetitions combined with conviction will help you reprogram yourself with a much better and healthier habit; a habit that supports you instead of holding you back."

"So, five index cards," Neil summarized, "read it with feeling especially at night and keep at it until I make good posture a habit. This sounds cool, but will it work?"

"I guarantee you, Neil, if you believe it will work ... it will."

"Can I borrow a pen and some paper, Frank? I want to write this down before my horse makes me forget."

"WHY SOITENLY!"

Chapter Twenty-five

"Hey Gramps, I think I'll go down and practice my rowing awhile." It was mid-afternoon. Brian decided to practice before his family arrived so he could take his mother and little sister for a cruise around the lake. "I need to work on my stroke and do a better job turning."

Frank was busy setting up an outdoor shower. "Sure thing, Boyo, I'll finish up with this and walk down in a little bit. Have fun."

Brian walked down to the boat. It remained where they'd left it, pulled up on the shore. However, it was nearly half full of rainwater. The plastic jug, life jackets and bucket floated inside the boat along with a variety of other things. Brian recalled his grandfather explaining how the drain plug worked so he removed it to empty the water from the boat. Brian soon had the plug replaced, the boat tidy and ready to launch.

He pushed the small craft down into the lake. Carefully he stepped in and made his way toward the stern. When he stepped over the first seat he felt wobbly, but by grabbing the side of the boat he steadied himself. 'The gun-als is what they are called not the sides; funny word, its spelled g-u-n-w-a-l-e-s.' Brian used one of the oars to push the boat clear of the shore and poled out toward the middle of Fish Lake. As soon as he felt he was in water deep enough to row he set the oars in the oarlocks. He took a moment to review what he'd been taught about rowing. He was aware of how the oars should feel in his hand and how the stroke worked to move the boat through the water. As he eagerly began rowing, Brian paid particular attention to his technique. The rowboat glided through the water, leaving small ripples in its wake.

Frank made the last adjustment to the shower. 'It's all set. I'll fill it up tomorrow and we'll all have an easy way to wash the dust off.'

He liked the way the small tarp provided a little privacy. Humming an old Irish tune, Frank felt happy and contented. 'This trip has been great. Brian has been a joy and we've already shared several memorable experiences. The day after tomorrow the rest of the family arrives and I'll get to see my son, my daughter-in-law and my darling granddaughter.'

Frank walked toward the lake and suddenly realized they had not gotten any wood. 'There are just a few pieces of wood left over from last night; we'd better do something about that before too long.' Frank walked along enjoying the scenery. He spotted a well-worn trail on the north side of the road. 'I'll bet this'll take me to the dock.'

The path led Frank toward the water and then near the shoreline. At times, he could see Brian rowing the boat. However, for the most part a screen of trees and brush obscured his view of the lake. So, when he finally arrived at the dock he was pleased to see his grandson rowing smoothly toward him. Brian's back was turned away from him but Frank could sense his grandson felt relaxed. 'His stroke is way smoother and it looks like he's having fun.'

Just on the other side of the boat ramp was a middle-aged couple sitting in folding chairs. The man fished, his line stretched out to a bright red and white float. The woman sat quietly holding a soft drink in one hand and a worn paperback in her other. Covering her head and neck, was a large floppy hat. It was yellow with red flowers. There were two more people fishing from the dock; next to a very old man sat a young boy. 'They're using bait with bobbers. I guess that'll work here.'

When Frank stepped onto the dock, the old man turned to him and nodded. Turning back to the lake, he said to the young boy, "Better reel in, Jason, or this kid will row over our lines."

Frank looked up and realized the old man was right. In a few more strokes Brian would indeed cross their lines. He called loudly to his grandson, "Hey, Brian, slow down for a wee minute; let these gentlemen reel in or you'll foul their lines."

Brian turned his head at the sound of Frank's voice. At once he saw the situation he was causing. He immediately did a powerful back stroke which effectively stopped the boat. Turning his body slightly, he apologized. "Sorry, I didn't realize I was so close ... sorry."

The old man replied, "Don't worry about it, son, it's not like we're catchin' anything. Reelin' in is the most action we've had all morning. Besides, it's about time we checked our bait."

Frank spoke quietly, "That's mighty nice of you, sir, thank you."

"Don't mention it." He turned again toward Frank and with a nod at Brian asked, "Your grandson?"

"Yes."

The old man looked at Frank with clear blue eyes, his wrinkled skin tanned, almost leathery. A navy baseball cap rested upon his head, the words 'USS Missouri' written upon it. Frank wondered if the old man was a veteran of World War II. 'I'll bet he is; he's sure about the right age.' The boy sitting next to the old man finished reeling in and held up his pole. The hook dangled a couple of feet below the bobber. The bait was gone. "Stupid fish; they stole my worm again, Popo."

"They'll do that. Let's bait up and wait for this young man to get that boat out of the way."

Frank cleared his throat slightly and asked, "Is this your grandson?"

The old man grunted and without looking up replied, "Great-grandson ... Jason."

"Hi, Jason, I'm Frank. No luck, huh?"

"Nope, they steal the bait."

Frank asked the old man, "Were you on the Mighty Mo?"

A Good Deed

"Nope ... visited it once when it was in Portland. I served on a tanker. Spent four years in the Navy and never heard an angry shot. One time our convoy was attacked by a Jap sub. I heard about it the next day." The old man grunted again. "Looks like your boy is goin' to try dockin' it ... been watching him practice. He's gettin' the hang of it, but this should be interesting."

Brian had indeed decided to row the boat to the dock. 'I'm aimed that way already, and with all the practicing I've been doing, Gramps will be impressed.' He pulled slowly to get the small craft moving. He knew he wanted to approach the dock from the side, so, he told himself, 'I need to go this way before swinging round which should bring me alongside the dock.' Brian concentrated as he pushed with his left hand and pulled with his right. 'Good, it's going where I wanted it to.' After a few strokes, Brian thought it time to begin turning.

He had just set himself to turn the rowboat northward when he heard a deep, gravelly voice bark out. "Too soon! Take another soft stroke, then turn."

The voice left no room for doubt. Brian took another stroke as he'd been told. Taking a quick look over his shoulder, he could see his grandfather standing on the dock with the old man and the boy. They were all looking at him. Brian realized he had to turn right away. He pushed hard with his right hand and pulled with the left. The small boat responded. It straightened out just in time for him to take one last stroke before he shipped the oars. The side of the boat slid into the dock with a loud bump. The old man reached down and steadied it. He said, "That wasn't too bad, son."

"Thank you."

Frank had moved to the end of the dock and reached down into the boat and grabbed the rope from the bow. Using it, he secured the bow to a cleat on the dock. He turned to his grandson, "Brian, use the other rope to tie up the stern."

"Sure thing, Gramps."

With the boat tied up, Brian got out with a helping hand from his grandfather. "Thanks Gramps," and to the old man added, "And thank you sir, for your help. I'm sorry I almost ran over your lines."

"No matter son, no harm done."

"Hey Gramps, I need to go to the bathroom. I'll be right back."

Frank watched Brian walk briskly toward the outhouse before turning back to address the old man. "He is bound and determined to learn how to row a boat."

"He's learning; he'll get it."

Jason held up his line. A worm dangled from his hook. "Hey, Popo, how's this?"

"Looks good son. Now, fish over there so's the boat won't bother it when he shoves off." The old man nodded beyond the stern of the boat.

"Okay." The boy cast in the direction indicated. The float splashed some 20 feet from the dock. He sat in silence while the old man baited his hook.

"If we don't catch something soon, Jason, we might as well go on back to camp. We can always try again later."

Frank heard the door of the outhouse slam shut. He looked up to see Brian walking back in his direction. Frank stepped off the dock and took a few steps toward his grandson. "You seem to be gettin' better at rowing. Havin' fun?"

"You bet. Hey, do you want to fish? I'll row and you can troll."

Frank thought for a moment before replying, "No, Boyo, I've fished enough for a while. You just practice and when you're done we'll go find firewood. Okay?"

They turned toward the dock. Brian said, "But I wanted to try rowing while you fished. You know, trolling seems like ... well like, rowing with a purpose."

A Good Deed

Frank laughed, "Yes, it is rowing with a purpose, but really … I've fished enough."

Brian shrugged his shoulders. 'He doesn't want to fish. Darn, I wanted to troll. Wait a second!' Brian had an idea. "Hey Gramps, would it be okay if I took this kid and the old man fishing? You know, they might catch some fish trolling. They're not doin' any good from the dock."

"That's very considerate of you, Brian. Let's ask them." Frank was happy that Brian wanted to help. It showed him that Brian had an awareness and compassion for others that Frank was glad to see. "We've got the life jackets in the boat, right?"

"Yep, Gramps, they're there."

Frank explained to the old man what Brian had in mind. Jason was visibly excited at the prospect of going for a boat ride. The old man nodded knowingly. He cleared his throat, "I guess it'll be okay. I haven't been in a rowboat for many a year. Why not? Thank you, son, that's mighty nice of you."

So after the old man and the boy changed their set-ups from worms to lures, Frank helped them into the small boat. He untied the stern after helping Brian get in.

He cast off the bowline and knelt on the deck, and, grasping the dock with his left hand, he shoved the boat with his other. It glided away from the dock. He smiled as he watched his grandson row. Brian headed for the middle of the lake. The old man and the young boy sat in the stern fishing. Frank heard Brian talking to them, but couldn't hear what was said.

He stood on the dock watching the progress of the boat as it made its way around the lake. He felt happy and proud. 'Brian is sure a nice kid. He's thoughtful and considerate.'

His thoughts were interrupted however, when he heard the woman in the chair say in a loud voice, "Aw, Dave, I thought you were quitting. Those things will kill you." Frank looked over to where the couple sat to see the man lighting up a cigarette.

The man responded, "I will when I want to … besides, it hasn't killed me yet."

His answer suddenly reminded Frank of an argument he'd had with Robert years before. They were in a parking lot. Frank had happened upon Robert smoking a cigarette and had unloaded on him. A pasty-faced man nearby was also smoking and intruded in the conversation saying almost the same thing, "I've been smoking for 30 years. It hasn't killed me yet."

Frank remembered feeling confused at the time. He didn't have a ready reply and stammered something to Robert. His son used the interruption as a chance to walk off in a huff. Frank recalled the loathing he had felt toward the pasty-faced smoker. He'd wanted to say things like, 'Who cares if you live or die' or 'Shut up, you asshole,' but said nothing. Later, replaying the whole thing in his mind, Frank had come up with a much more appropriate answer, but of course he never had a chance to voice it.

He thought of how he felt then. He even thought of saying to this man what he'd failed to say to the pasty-faced smoker all those years ago but decided not to. 'It's none of my business. If someone wants to smoke that's their problem.' Frank turned from the couple and looked to the lake. 'I wonder how Brian is doing.'

Brian rowed slowly. After the initial excitement of getting their lines in the water the fishermen had settled in quietly. The old man turned in his seat and said, "Your grandfather called you Brian. Is that right?"

"Yes sir."

"I'm Bill and this here is Jason. Thanks again for doin' this."

Brian replied with a phrase he'd heard his grandfather say, "It's a pleasure to be of service."

A Good Deed

"I've got one Popo! I've got one!" Jason's pole was bent and the line moved to the left.

Bill grunted and started to reel in his line when suddenly his pole bent as well. "I've got one too, Jason! Fish on!"

Brian stopped rowing in order to allow them to land their fish. As soon as both fish were in the boat and Bill and Jason were ready to fish again, he began to row. He made a slow S-turn and looked around. They were nearing the area that Frank had told him contained a good hole. He pulled a little harder. The boat sped up and almost immediately Jason caught another fish. This fish was added to the bucket and before too long, the boy caught his third fish.

Bill patted Jason on his head and tussled his hair. "Oh, boy! Now we're havin' fun! I better get busy here or you're gonna catch all the fish in the lake."

Jason laughed. He quickly got his line back into the water and waited for the next fish to strike. But the next fish was Bill's.

"Fish on! Oh, boy, this one's a big one." When he brought the fish up to the boat, Bill used the net to bring it in. It proved to be just slightly bigger than the others, so Jason had to say something about whose fish was the biggest. Bill responded with a grunt and a laugh, "You don't measure the fish, till the fishin' is done."

Listening to their banter, Brian smiled and felt glad to have helped. It didn't take long before both Bill and Jason had caught five fish each. Brian said, as Bill added his last fish to the bucket, "Well, that's the limit for both of you. I guess we can head back."

"Son, that was the most fun fishin' I've had in a long, long time. Thank you. Say thank you to Brian, Jason."

"Thank you, Brian, that was great!"

"It was my pleasure."

"I can't wait to get back and tell my dad," Jason said excitedly.

Brian smiled as he started back to the dock. He settled into a smooth rhythm.

Bill spoke softly to Brian. He explained, in some detail, the workings of rowboats. The way he spoke led Brian to realize he was speaking to Jason as well. He finished with, "When you get really good at rowing, each stroke affects the line ... how fast ... how straight ... it changes when you wish it to change through an almost unconscious change in how your hands grip the oars and how your power is fed through them. You learn to take the basic skill of rowing and raise it up to ... well, almost an art form."

As soon as Bill said this it occurred to Brian that it made sense. It felt correct. Brian knew now what the final stage of learning was! He knew and it seemed fitting to him.

Frank watched as the boat made its way around the lake. He saw the first fish brought into the boat. He could hear, muffled by distance and wind, the laughter and the excitement. He wondered how his grandson felt as he maneuvered the small boat over the placid waters of Fish Lake. He felt proud of Brian for offering to guide strangers to where they could enjoy catching some fish. He also noted the generations represented by those in the boat and was glad.

Bill talked Brian into the dock. It went much better this time, the boat gliding easily up to the dock. They soon had it tied up. Frank helped Bill and Jason get back on the dock. Jason jabbered excitedly about all the fish they'd caught as only a nine-year old boy would. He described for Frank each fish and how it was caught. Frank smiled at Jason and winked at Brian.

To Brian he said, "That's great! It took just about 40 minutes for them to limit out, which is a good thing, Boyo 'cause we still have to go find some firewood."

Bill, who had started off the dock with Jason, stopped at the mention of firewood, and turned to Frank. "You guys need firewood?"

Frank nodded yes. "Yep, we sure do. I looked around yesterday and found very little. I sure wish I'd brought some."

Bill cleared his throat. "We got plenty. My son brought his chain saw and we found a nice, dry slash pile not too far from here. We've got more'n we can use. Which campsite are you in?"

Slightly embarrassed, Frank replied, "Uh, 22, but you don't—"

"Nonsense." Bill's gravelly voice cut in, "This time it will be our pleasure."

Without having to go find wood, Frank and Brian decided to go for a drive after dinner. They drove back toward Frenchglen for a few miles until Frank spotted a small dirt road. He turned onto it. It ran south through a small marshy meadow that sported wildflowers in bloom. The narrow road then wound through a grove of aspen before ending in a larger meadow of sagebrush and juniper. When they first drove into this larger meadow they startled a small herd of mule deer. The pair watched in amazement as the deer took flight, their large, graceful leaps taking them quickly into the trees on the far side of the meadow and out of sight.

When they reached a dead end, Frank turned around and drove back to the main road. Then they turned east and drove beyond the campground. As they crested the ridgeline of the Steens, the sun began to set in the west. Rain clouds to the southwest began to turn a bright pink. The rain in the distance was clearly visible. The setting sun illuminated both the clouds and the falling rain with a palette of pastels. Frank stopped and got out. He walked to the front of the truck and watched. Brian joined him. They stood and watched in silence as the colors of the sunset changed from pink to red to a deep red, then finally to purple.

The sun set completely. The clouds now cast a steel-gray shadow against the early night sky. Brian sighed. He said, "Wow, Gramps that was amazing!"

"Yes Brian, it was. From up here you sure can see for a long, long way. I remember coming up here with your grandmother once to watch a sunset. It was pretty, but tonight was spectacular, wasn't it?"

"It sure was."

"This was a sunset I'll never forget. Way up here ... it's like you can see forever."

"Yeah ... hey Gramps, have you ever come up here to ... to ah, you know, watch a sunrise?"

"You know Brian, I never have seen a dawn from up here; that's a really good idea. Do you want to see what it's like tomorrow?"

"Sure."

On the drive back to camp Frank enjoyed the thought of coming up to see dawn from the rim with its magnificent eastward view. He also thought of two quotes that he'd bring along. He couldn't wait.

When they got back to camp, Frank built a rather large fire. They sat around it and talked of the trip so far. Frank could tell Brian was enjoying himself. The fire burned down to coals before Brian stood up and added more wood. The fire flared up. He hadn't been back in his seat for more than a couple of minutes before they heard Neil's voice: "Hey Brian ... hello, Frank, what's up?"

Frank looked up at the sound of the greeting. Neil and Vanessa entered the firelight. "Well, welcome back. To what do we owe the honor?"

Neil started to answer but Vanessa who seemed to be excited spoke first. "We were talking about those re-affirmations and we came up with a great idea!"

A Good Deed

Neil added, "Yeah, we thought about something … so, we thought we'd come over to tell you about it."

Brian asked, "What is it?"

"Neil was talking about his standing tall re-affirmation … oh, by the way, why isn't it just called an affirmation?"

Frank answered, "It would be an affirmation the first time you said it but every time after that it would be more accurate to call it a re-affirmation, wouldn't it?"

"Yeah, I guess … but anyway, where was I—oh, yeah … could you come up with a re-affirmation that would be good for restaurant workers to say?"

"That is an intriguing idea, young lady … go on."

"Well, we were talking about how kids who … you know … work in a restaurant could change their attitude about their jobs, but we …" She hesitated.

Neil continued, "We thought you might help."

Frank looked at Brian before answering, "Why don't we all sit here and see if we can come up with something good, huh?"

Brian quickly agreed. Frank stood and retrieved two more camp chairs. He handed one to Neil and set up the other for Vanessa. "Let's talk about it."

Frank sat and mostly listened as the kids discussed what a good re-affirmation for restaurant workers might sound like. When they were stuck on the exact definition of what good customer service was, Frank guided the discussion with a few pointed questions, but let the youngsters arrive at their own answers. After a while Frank was happy to see that they not only seemed to grasp the concept of drafting an effective re-affirmation but actually came up with one. Vanessa summarized, "So, I'm a restaurant worker and this is what I want to believe … I always provide our customers with the kind of service that exceeds their wishes. Good customer service helps our customers, my employer and my co-workers. Doing my best honors the customer and allows me to establish a habit of excellence for myself. I do this to set a good example for my friends and co-workers. Is that it?"

Brian replied, "Yeah ... that sounds right. Is there anything else?"

"I'll bet my uncle is gonna love this."

Frank sat back in his chair. "Any restaurant owner would want his employees to have that as a belief. Neil, you're right."

"This whole process of writing a re-affirmation is cool," Vanessa added. "Tell me Frank, do you do these all the time?"

Frank thought for a minute. "Why, I can't remember the last time I wrote a new one. It must be years since I used this technique to change a habit or attitude of mine."

Brian looked puzzled. "But, Gramps, if it works so well, why don't you use it all the time?"

"Good question, Boyo ... I don't know ... guess I haven't felt the need to change something in a long time."

Brian sat silently before he spoke. "What you really mean is you're not aware of an attitude you want to change, right?"

"Exactly."

"But why not?" asked Vanessa.

Frank answered, "Why not, indeed."

The kids continued their discussion. Their youthful fervor brought a smile to Frank's face, but he kept thinking. 'It has been years since I've used this myself. I know I've shared it at least a few times over the years, but it hasn't occurred to me to write a new one for myself until tonight. Hmmm ... what would I want to change?'

Frank was lost in thought until Brian asked him a question. "Huh, Brian, what was that?"

"I said, 'Can you use this to correct any attitude?' "

"I suppose so. I've used it with success to change my listening habits, to help me fall asleep easily and to get into the habit of wearing my seat belt all the time. You kids raise an interesting point."

A shower of sparks accompanied by a loud pop drew everyone's attention to the fire. Brian and Neil returned to the discussion about wanting to change habits. They debated while Vanessa listened. Frank returned to his thoughts.

After a while Neil yawned, stood up and stretched. "It's time we got back ... I'm beat and want to get to bed."

Vanessa agreed, "Yeah, me too. I'm exhausted."

After they left, Frank and Brian sat in front of the fire. Brian moved his chair so that he could see his grandfather's face. He wanted to talk about what he'd read in Frank's Bulletin Board. They talked about many things, including quotes on success and happiness. As the fire burned down, the light shimmered on their faces.

Brian asked, "Hey, Gramps, what's up with you and my dad not talkin' to each other for so long? I mean ... he's your son and all. How come you and my dad spent so much time being mad at each other?"

"That is something I've been spending a lot of time thinking about, Brian." Frank sat back in his chair. He looked up at the stars before continuing. "I think in the days following your grandmother's death ... well, it was tough on everyone. I ... we ... all felt lost. Anyway, I retreated into what I can only describe today as auto-pilot. I was their dad, but only on the surface ... you know ... the daily stuff of life, dinner, work, school ... like that. I couldn't even begin to come to grips with my own grief over losing my wife; never mind trying to empathize with my children, who'd lost their mother." Frank's voice broke. "I believe I got lost at a time when my kids could have used more support and understanding than I had to give." He felt himself getting choked up. He took a few deep breaths. "Whatever Robert and Mary were going through ... well, anyway ... I didn't seek to understand. When I found out that

Robert was smoking cigarettes, I went nuts. I said the same things over and over, louder and louder, as if by saying them louder would make him listen to me. That just flat-out doesn't work." Frank fell silent.

"You miss Grandma, don't you?"

"Terribly; I loved her very much. I love my son and daughter too, yet spent far too long not talking to my son. The bottom line is this: the only way family members can stay that angry with each other is if one or both of them refuses to live by the Golden Rule or they just don't care. Sometimes, I suppose, it's easier not to. But I never stopped caring and I don't think your dad did either. We simply got in the habit of avoiding each other. A big part of 'doing unto others' requires understanding the others' point of view. How else can you know what they would want? My lack of empathy led to miscommunication and hurt feelings that I truly regret. I never want to let anything like that happen again."

Brian poked at the fire. He rolled a log near him closer to the others. He reflected on what his grandfather had said. He knew his dad and how important his family was to him. He now knew his grandfather well enough to know that 'family' was important to him as well. He wondered, 'How could this have ever happened?'

"Gramps, if you had a chance to go back in time and change some things about those days, what would you want to change?"

"That's a good question, Brian, I suppose … wait—why, that's brilliant!" Frank started to answer before suddenly realizing where Brian's line of thought would lead him. "What attitudes did I have … what beliefs did I have … what habits did I have back then that prevented me from really listening! If I don't figure out what I felt then, I can't really change. Here I am trying to explain things to you and it's you who taught me."

"I have? Well good. Okay then, what's next?"

A Good Deed

"Well, I need to identify the limiting things and replace them with enabling things."

"Things? Things? Oh, now you're getting all technical on me."

Frank leaned forward and laughed. "Yeah I know, okay. It's like finding out what the problem is and then discovering what the opposite of it is. Well, maybe not so much the opposite as 'the versus' of it. Oh, I'm not being real clear. Okay, back then I was ... let's call it heartsick. I was grieving and I stayed focused on my own loss for far too long. If I could have had more empathy, I might have done better. Oh, I still would have grieved, but maybe it wouldn't have lasted as long or I might have been more effective in dealing with my kids while I grieved."

"This sounds like a bunch of what ifs."

"Yeah it does sound like that, but really ... if you can identify what you believed then, you have a chance to change the way you feel today. If you can change the way you feel today, you can be more effective. You can deal with similar situations better. You can learn to be happier."

"Happier?"

"Well yes, isn't happiness an attitude?"

"I guess. So okay, what would a new re-affirmation sound like?"

"That's the question. Let's see, how does this work? I take the time to try to understand the other people involved in my life and acknowledge their point of view. I always understand the emotional elements in each situation. To those I love, I extend every possible courtesy."

"That sounds good; is that it?"

"I don't know. When I've done these in the past I'd try it on for a while and if I couldn't improve it, well then, I'd write it up. This one may take quite a lot of tweaking."

"Tweaking?"

"Yeah. You know, adjusting ... you evaluate it and you change it until you can't improve it any more. For example, in this case you might analyze the words to make sure you are using precisely the right word in the right way. Or you might examine the concept you're trying for, to make sure that it's correct." Frank could see questions in Brian's face. He continued, "So you have those two elements, the words and the concept ... you know, I wanted to talk to you about words anyway, so let's start with them.

"There is a great novel written by John Steinbeck entitled *East of Eden*. Steinbeck tells how Lee, the Chinese servant, explores the true meaning behind the translations of the Hebrew word 'timshel' in the Bible. What got Lee excited was the effect different translations made in the same passage. In one interpretation 'thou shall overcome evil' suggests it's preordained. In another interpretation, 'do thou overcome evil' suggests it's something God commanded. Lee discovered 'timshel' is the Hebrew word for 'thou mayest.' Well, 'thou mayest overcome evil' means that the choice is up to you ... the choice is yours to make and it is never too late to choose good."

Frank sat back in his chair. "This story within the book captured my attention. The thing I realized about words is that we use them to describe things but they are not the things themselves. We use them to describe the landscape but they are not the landscape. A certain word may mean one thing to one person, and something a little different to another. Change a word in a sentence, and even if you use a synonym, you change the sentence. So, it's crucial to choose your words carefully. The whole thing I do on words, you know, like when I asked you to look up 'honor' in the dictionary, that whole process comes from this book. I think it is a great way to analyze something. Break it down into its most simple, basic form, then look at each part and put it back together. This same technique can be used to improve a skill, and I don't think it is a coincidence that it works for both."

"I was surprised to see all the different ways that 'honor' can be defined."

"Exactly; not only that, but sometimes you might arrive at a different conclusion about what something means based upon a broader interpretation. I know! Listen to this ... 'Honor thy Father and thy Mother.' I'm sure you recognize that as one of the Ten Commandments."

"Yeah ...?"

"The way it was taught to me, it meant to obey your parents and respect them. Right?"

"Yeah, that's right," Brian answered.

"Okay, what if we took a different approach to 'honor'. What if the intention of this commandment is to tell us we must do our best? And, by doing our best, THAT is how we 'honor' those who gave us life. Now that's a much different take on it, don't you think?"

"Yeah, so you should make sure you're using exactly the right word in your re-affirmation. So, what do you mean by the right concept?"

"You helped with Neil's re-affirmation. You know, we decided that he needed to replace his slouching habit with something better, right?"

"Yeah ... his standing tall habit?"

"Exactly. We didn't replace it with a non-slouching habit; we picked standing tall. This is a very important distinction. By finding the right new habit we are able to change the old habit. You want to find something that's like the opposite of what you're trying to replace. Maybe the idea of versus is better than opposite. Standing tall versus slouching ... I don't know if I'm being real clear on this. Let me think about it and we'll talk about it later."

"Okay."

Brian leaned back in his chair and looked up. The crescent moon hung overhead. The brightest stars were easily visible, but Brian knew that the best stargazing would happen after the moon set. He looked back to the fire and watched the heat from the glowing coals dance and move. He thought about what his grandfather had talked about. Going through the Bulletin Board and talking to Frank raised a lot of questions. "Gramps, you seem to know a lot of stuff ... can I ask you about something?"

"Certainly."

"How ... well, what I ... can you explain to me about girls?"

"You want to know about females? Sorry, Boyo, I can't help you much. Who knows what goes through the mind of a woman? If you figure it out, please let me know, okay?"

"Yeah, I guess." Brian answered in a disappointed manner.

"The best advice I have for you in that area is this: it is far more important for you to become comfortable talking with girls than anything else. Everything else follows from there. If you try to be friends with girls you'll find it just gets easier and easier to get to know them and eventually you'll figure things out okay."

"What about, you know ... love?"

"Love? Why, you've got plenty of time for that, Boyo; don't rush it. It will happen for you when the time is right."

"How do you know when you're in love?"

"I think that's different for everyone. When the part of you that needs a special connection to someone else demands your attention and when you find someone you feel is lovable, you'll connect. I don't want to make this sound like it's easy or anything. It's not that simple. But the better you know the other person in a relationship the better your chances of finding happiness."

"Well, um ... you know Sarah, right? Well I really thought ... she's really cute and er ... I like her. What should I do?"

"As soon as you get back make sure you contact her. Just say 'hi,' or better yet, send her the photos from Watson Falls and a short note. If she's interested, she'll reply. You can take it from there. One thing I can tell you is girls want to get to know you too. They want to see what you're like and what your interests are. They want to find out what kind of person you are, you know, like your personality, your character, stuff like that."

"But what if we do like each other?"

"Just take it one step at a time. Don't be in a rush. Girls worry when the guy seems like he's in a hurry. They worry ... he might be ... how do I say this, might be—"

"Trying to trick her?" Brian finished Frank's thought.

"Exactly."

"Okay." Brian got up and added another piece of wood to the fire. He watched as the flames sprang up. Tongues of red, yellow and gold danced around the wood. The coals beneath glowed. He sat back down and let his mind wander.

"Hey, Gramps," he said after several minutes, "Do you have any kind of general advice for me, you know, about stuff?"

Frank laughed at the word stuff. "There is a lot of good 'stuff' in the Bulletin Board. If I would add anything to what we've already talked about, what would it be? Let's see ... live your life like you're important. It's an attitude that will help you. Read good books; look for the lessons not only in books but in movies, in songs and in your day-to-day living. Never forget the influence you have on others. Like a stone thrown into a pond, you make ripples. Be grateful for your life. And remember: life is a journey, enjoy it."

"It's weird; I never thought about my life affecting others."

"Your life will affect many others just as many others have affected your life. You know, Brian, sitting here in front of a fire, the stars overhead, reminds me of something I think about from time to time. Those stars we see up there are really old. Why, the light from many of those stars is tens of thousands of years old. The light takes so long to reach us that the star itself may no longer even exist, but we still see the energy it generated all those years ago. When I look up and see all those stars, it makes me wonder what our ancestors thought when they looked up at the night sky. It wasn't all that long ago that they would have been part of a tribe of people who lived by hunting and gathering, by hard, unrelenting work. They survived long enough to pass down their legacy to us. Do you know what legacy I'm talking about?"

"Life?"

"Exactly, life. We are here because our ancestors did whatever it took to survive. Look, for example we're Irish, well at least part Irish, right?"

"Yeah."

"Both of my grandparents came to this country from Ireland after the turn of the century, which means that on both sides they were descended from people who survived the Great Potato Famine. Anyone with European roots is here today because someone had the good luck to have survived the Black Plague."

"All of us alive today owe our existence ... our very lives ... to those ancestors. I tell you Brian, we stand on the shoulders of giants. Sometimes I like to think of our ancestors watching us ... seeing what we're doing ... you know, how we live, how we handle things. We are alive today because of them. We are alive here and now ... it's our time now. How will you live?"

A Good Deed

Chapter Twenty-Six

Brian rubbed the sleep from his eyes as he stepped out of the camper. Standing in predawn darkness, he took a few steps and looked up. Stars filled the sky. The moon had already set and there was, as yet, no hint of sunrise. He'd never seen so many stars. The Milky Way was plainly visible. It reminded him of a kind of mist floating across the darkness. Brighter stars were surrounded by uncountable smaller ones. 'At least two of those bright ones are planets. Let's see, that must be Venus. It's easily the brightest thing in the sky. That one must be Mars; it's got a red tint to it.' While Brian rarely found himself awake at three-thirty on any morning, here at Fish Lake, he was glad he was.

"Hey, Gramps, look at all those stars! This is incredible!"

Frank locked the camper door and stepped down to join his grandson. They stood enjoying the celestial show. Just then, the pair saw a brilliant shooting star dart above them in the southeastern sky as it slashed northward leaving a long tail.

Brian laughed and said with emphasis, "Sa-weeet!"

Frank patted his grandson on the back and said, "Yes it is. Let's load up and get a move on. I want get up to the rim well before daybreak."

"Fine with me, Gramps."

Frank pulled the truck into the parking area at the Steens Summit with plenty of time to spare. "Sunrise is still at least a half-hour away. Will you look at this view!"

Stars spilled across the horizon. The moments before dawn were not darkest at all, but instead filled with light. Starlight shone down upon them as the travelers stood and watched. Brian looked up and slowly turned counterclockwise.

"Wow!"

"Hey, Boyo, there's a satellite. See, it's moving southwest ... right there." Frank pointed overhead.

"Yeah, I see it. Hey, Gramps, does standing up here make you feel small?"

Frank answered absentmindedly, "It's funny, but I think being here makes me feel small and big, both at the same time."

"Yeah, I know what you mean."

Slowly the faint glow on the horizon brightened. The dark band of night moved ever so slightly upward. The brightest stars were still visible, but others surrendered to the coming morning. The two stood watching. They were spectators to the beginning of a new day. Frank pulled some papers from inside his jacket. His voice startled Brian. "Less than a 100 miles west of here is a point where John C. Fremont once stood. It's called Fremont's Point. It may well have been the first time a white man saw this part of the world. The people who lived here, the Native Americans, had different beliefs than did the settlers that came later in such numbers, in such waves. Now that it's light enough I want to read something to you."

Brian said nothing. He waited for his grandfather to continue.

"This is an Apache blessing ... 'May the sun bring you energy by day: may the moon softly restore you by night: may the rain wash away your worries: may the breeze blow new strength into your being. May you walk gently through the world and know its beauty all the days of your life.' "

Brian nodded his head. The sun began to emit a salmon-colored glow on the tops of distant mountains. Around them the rocks and grasses became distinct. Brian began to see more detail in the desert below as well as the outline of mountaintops rooted in Idaho.

Frank shuffled another paper to the top. "These are quotes from Tecumseh, a Shawnee warrior chief." He cleared his throat. " 'So live your life that the fear of death can never enter your heart. Trouble no man about his religion – respect him in his views and demand that he respect yours. Love your life; perfect your life. Beautify all things in your life. Seek to make your life long and of service to your people. Show respect to all, but grovel to none. When you arise in the morning, give thanks for the morning light, for your life and strength. Give thanks for your food and for the joy of living. If you see no reason for giving thanks, the fault is yours.' "

In the east the light grew brighter. The night retreated grudgingly. As Brian watched, silent and expectant, the first rays of sunlight crept over the distant horizon, casting a pinkish glow. The mountains below took on a purple haze. He gave thanks.

After a long while he spoke. "Gramps, do you ever feel like you're part of a place, like you know, like you belong there?"

Frank reflected before answering, "Who is to say that a place not only affects you as you see it, alive in a moment of your life, enjoying it, but that something of you touches the place. Who has not stood, say at the seashore, staring at the ocean, mesmerized by the flashings of brilliant light upon dancing waves, only to be distracted by a seagull or a pretty woman, each borne by unseen currents, each moved in that moment of existence to be there ... with you as witness."

"Whoa! What the ... I don't get that at all."

Frank answered in his raspy Yoda voice, "Only when ready you are, will you understand the true nature of the Force."

"Very funny, but no, really?"

"Sometimes there are lessons we must be ready for, you know, before we understand the real message. Think about it."

"Whatever you say," Brian said doubtfully.

They watched the rest of the dawn, the sun rising above the mountains, shadows shrinking along the desert floor. Wisps of clouds wore morning shades of purple and red and pink before turning white. What were once dark patches in the landscape became green. Quietly they got back into the truck and returned to camp.

Frank sat in a comfortable chair with his legs resting on the cold stones of the fire pit. "Brian, one of the great delights of camping is taking the traditional mid-morning nap. I feel it's vital that you get the full camping experience." He pulled his hat down over his eyes.

Within minutes, Brian heard him snoring. Brian felt impressed at his grandfather's ability to fall asleep. 'I've never seen anyone go to sleep so easily.' He went into the camper, crawled into bed and in a short time was also asleep.

When they woke up, Brian needed to think so he decided to hike to the canyon of the Blitzen River. After he'd left, Frank felt like going for a swim. He carried a towel down to the lake and hung it, with his shirt, on a branch before stepping into the lake.

Frank felt the mud at the bottom of the lake as it squished around his toes. A branch or stick became stuck between his toes, but by pulling his foot back, he was able to dislodge it. He remembered when he was young, going for a swim in a small lake in upstate New York when the same thing happened. The water here felt warmer than he expected. Down near his feet it was cooler and Frank began to anticipate a nice swim. He walked farther out past the vegetation.

His last few steps took Frank into deeper water. He decided to dive in. The water felt wonderful. After four or five powerful strokes he tried to stand. As he had guessed, he couldn't touch bottom. After treading water for a minute he pointed his arms above his head and slid below the surface. When he was fully submerged he used his arms to propel himself even deeper but quickly hit bottom. 'Hmmm, it's about nine feet deep here.'

As he broke the surface Frank flipped onto his back and swam for a short distance using a lazy backstroke. He switched to a frog kick just to keep moving. He looked up as he swam and smiled. The sky was bright blue with a scattering of high white clouds. They drifted lazily from the west, occasionally hiding the sun.

A feeling of peacefulness washed over him. He loved swimming. How many days, when he was young, were spent in the ocean? He recalled playing in the surf with his friends. They would body surf, taking in wave after wave, trying to ride the best ones; the longest rides brought them right up to where the little kids played. The waves surrounded, supported, and carried them. They became smaller and smaller until as mere ripples they would wash up onto shore. So, what started out as a ride on a big powerful wave could end in inches of water, quietly and serenely. Frank loved that feeling of quiet as the ride ended. It always seemed a fitting end to a good ride. Of course, as soon as one wave ended, the surfer would spring up and race back, dodging waves and swimmers in a mad dash to get in position for the next big wave. 'Ah, those were the days.'

Frank flipped over onto his stomach and kicked. He swam for a short distance before doing a surface dive. He swam under water. He kept his eyes open but the water was murky, the visibility limited. He looked up and saw a blanket of sunshine covering the water. This too, brought him back to a time when he was young. He was rising to the surface with the light shining through the top of a wave as it broke over him. The smooth feel of the water as it whooshed over his body delighted him. It was as if he became part of the water, one with the ocean. This led him to remember being afraid of sharks, but the more he learned about the creatures, the easier it became to control that fear.

Now, as he broke the surface of Fish Lake, he laughed at his memories of the ocean and of sharks. 'There are no sharks in this water. I'm the biggest thing swimming in this lake.' He swam easily. It occurred to him that sharks had to keep swimming or they died. 'When plants stop growing they die. Well, I'm still swimming. Am I still growing?' Suddenly, thoughts raced through his mind. He felt an intense clarity. 'I am still growing. I'm not dead yet! I feel so alive ... wait! My story isn't written yet!' Frank understood deeply the joy that Ebenezer Scrooge felt on that magical Christmas morning; the joy became part of him, enveloped him and infused him with its essence. 'Enjoy your life! Of course, isn't that what I've been telling Brian? Isn't that what Meg was telling me?'

Frank did another surface dive, this time swimming deeper. The deeper he swam, the colder the water felt. Just when Frank started to feel pressure in his ears, he turned up. Again, thoughts rushed into his awareness; they came to him unbidden and urgent.

Beneath the filtered sunlight, as if lost in the fog of time, he felt himself drawn toward the light, toward life; he felt his ancestors cheering him onward, toward his destiny, toward his purpose. He felt whole again. Now, he knew. He knew! He must enjoy his life because life is a gift to be enjoyed! He must be open to life. He realized that life was both the prize and the price of admission. Oh my God! He saw; he understood; life is to be lived ... life is to be enjoyed! Embrace the journey! Live with every breath!

Frank reached the surface. He sucked fresh air into his lungs. He inhaled life. He felt an overwhelming sense of joy and peace. He flipped over onto his back, looked up toward the sky and broke into song. "Jeremiah was a bullfrog ... was a good friend of mine ... never understood a single word he said ... but I helped him drink his wine ... yes, he always had some mighty fine wine ... sing it! joy to the world ... all the boys and girls now...joy to the fishes in the deep blue sea ... joy to you and me."

This sense of peace lasted well into the evening. They'd just finished some fruit for dessert; the rest of the hazelnut pie was being reserved until the whole family could enjoy it. Frank threw another log on the fire. "Would you look at how much wood those guys dropped off for us!" A large pile of firewood, neatly stacked near the fire pit, contained more than enough wood for a week's worth of camping. "That sure was nice of them, huh, Brian?"

"Yes, it was."

"Of course, it was really nice of you to take them out fishing. I guess sometimes, what goes around does come around. Kinda like karma."

Brian answered, "I guess." He looked into the fire with half-closed eyelids, brightness danced in yellow and red, bejeweled with sparks rising into the darkness. The oldest wood lay crumpled beneath the newer additions like fists of glowing fire. "Hey, Gramps, I would like to cook dinner tomorrow night. You know, for everybody."

"That's cool. What do you have in mind?"

"Well, I don't know ... something ... but I want to."

"Okay, then let's think about it. I expect them about noon or so. That leaves us time to fish ... you could take your mom and sister out like you did today and we could have fresh trout for dinner. What do you think about that?"

"Yeah, that'd be sweet." Brian wanted to help his sister and his mother catch fish. He wanted to fix dinner too, as a way of doing something for his family. He hoped to impress them.

"What else will you serve? Do you want help with the menu?"

"Sure, what else should I do?"

"Vegetables; we've got onions, peppers, tomatoes, corn ... oh, and I've got some zucchini ... we've got salad stuff along too ... then, biscuits or potatoes ... the pie for dessert."

"Okay, but how do I cook all that?"

"Well let's see ... sauté the trout in butter. You could spice things up a bit. I've got a recipe, Trout with Slivered Almonds. As I recall, we have all the ingredients." Frank ran down the list, "Slivered almonds, salt and pepper, garlic, onions, a half cup of white wine and of course the butter … the only thing we need is the trout."

"Don't worry about that," Brian said, "we'll have plenty of fish."

Frank suppressed a laugh. "Okay," he said doubtfully, "we'll see about that. Anyway, you could also serve sautéed veggies, biscuits and salad."

"And don't forget the pie for dessert."

"Of course not … what about coffee, too?"

"Yeah, sure … coffee sounds good. Do you have a coffee maker?"

"I do indeed, Boyo; I do indeed."

"No corn?"

"You could roast the corn in foil, but that's a lot of cookin' you're talkin' about. Are you sure you want to do all that work?"

Brian reached across the space between them and patted his grandfather's leg. "It will be an honor."

Nearer to sunset, a few scattered high clouds sailed across the sky, changing colors as the evening approached. One cloud, starting out as a pink flamingo, stretched by the wind, gradually became a blue heron as the sun slipped behind the mountains. In front of the fire, Frank relaxed into his chair. He braced his feet against the rocks.

Brian stepped down from the camper and joined him at the fire. He asked his grandfather, "Do you have anything special planned for when they get here?"

"Nothing set in stone. One day, I thought we might all head over to Nevada and loop around to the Alvord Desert, maybe on another day make a trip to the Hart Mountain Game Refuge."

"Oh, okay."

"Is there anything you want to do?"

"Ah, not really, just fish and whatever." Brian poked at the fire. He added two pieces of wood and moved them around until he achieved the perfect fire. He too sat back and put his feet up on the rocks. "Hey, Gramps, I've been thinking ... I want to change something. I ... um, want to do a re-affirmation. Will you help me?"

"Of course. Have you thought about what you'd like to change?"

"Yeah, I ... um want to be more sharing and uh, caring ... if you know what I mean."

Frank said nothing. He looked across the firelight to Brian and nodded.

"What I mean is, well, I think that sometimes I'm kinda shy and if I could have an attitude of wanting to share more of myself, well anyway ... that might help me not be so shy."

"Go on."

"I'm not always shy, you see, just sometimes with ... you know, girls."

"I see," Frank replied. "You're really talking about being more confident ... more open as well. I like how you framed it though ... sharing more of yourself. You want to be more outgoing, right?"

"Right. How do I write a re-affirmation for that?"

"I'll tell you what, Boyo, why don't you think a little more about this and together we'll come up with a good one. Okay?"

"Sure." Brian leaned forward. He folded his fingers together and rested his head on his hands. He stared into the fire. After a while he sat up abruptly. "Oh, I almost forgot! I told Neil I'd go over there after dinner." He stood up. "I won't be gone for long, Gramps."

Frank grinned. "Take your time. I'm glad you met those guys. They're nice kids. Don't be too late."

"I won't. They get to bed pretty early and besides, I'm tired. I want to get to bed early too."

Frank reflected on his grandson's re-affirmation. He was glad the boy wanted to write one. 'I think I can help him. He's willing to go through the process but is he clear on what he wants? We'll see. Is there a simpler way to say what he's going for? Hmmm, it's interesting that as a way to become more self-confident he chose to adopt an attitude of sharing. I have to give the boy credit for original thinking.'

Frank allowed his eyelids to close. He paid attention to his breathing. Each breath became part of an awareness and a release. Whenever thoughts bubbled up into his consciousness he allowed his focus to return to his breathing. Twenty minutes later Frank increased the rhythm of his breaths and opened his eyes.

The fire had burned down to a bed of glowing red embers. Frank gazed into the gently moving firelight and remembered his last big fight with Robert. Brian was still a baby. In his frustration, Frank had become angry. He lashed out at his son by wondering out loud what kind of an example Robert was setting for 'his' grandson. 'How dumb could I have been?' Frank shook his head in disbelief. Robert had replied with intensity, "I'm NEVER going to be good enough for you, am I?" Frank remembered very clearly saying the same thing to his father. When he heard Robert say those exact words to him, it seemed funny. Frank laughed at the coincidence but Robert became angrier and stormed off. Suddenly, Frank realized Robert might have thought Frank was laughing at him. 'How stupid of me, not to see this before! Robert thought I was laughing at him. I can't wait to ask him about this. Maybe we can finally put it behind us.'

He recalled the fight. 'Why was I so angry? Was it pride? Or self-righteousness? Or was I simply afraid of losing Robert too?'

Frank realized the truth at last. His basic fear lay exposed for him to see. He'd become afraid to lose what he loved, so he had kept those he loved at arm's length. 'Could Robert feel the same way?' Frank thought. 'And I haven't been able to feel comfortable with another woman because I'm afraid to lose what I love. I am afraid to love!'

Frank's thoughts were a jumble he couldn't sort out. 'In trying to explain how re-affirmations work I suddenly gain insight into myself. Brian wants to learn how to be more sharing and I find I've been afraid to share myself … God, its funny how life works sometimes. Robert thought I was dismissing him but it was just poor communication. How could I have been so blind?'

The sound of fluttering wings startled Frank. He looked up to see the last bit of twilight fleeing from the oncoming night. Nothing moved, yet he was sure he'd heard something. 'What the heck?' He stared at the sky for five or six minutes. 'There! What's that? There it is again. A bat! It's a bat hunting insects.' He laughed and said aloud, "Good, I'm not crazy … at least not yet."

'Okay,' thought Frank, 'where was I? Oh, yeah … I've identified the feelings I had. So what behavior do I want? Hmmm … patient and loving … if I could have a do-over, how would I wish to act? Well then, what would be a good re-affirmation? Let's see … Brian wishes to share more of himself … be more open. The kid may be onto something there.'

Frank mulled over a new self-affirmation: 'I am a good listener. I'm always patient, understanding and loving. These habits allow me to what? Show love? Share myself? What? These habits would be a great role-model for my loved ones. Nope…the whole thing needs tweaking. What am I trying to say?'

Standing up slowly, Frank stretched. He walked over to the wood pile and selected two small pieces. He placed one in the middle of the embers, stirred the coals with the other before adding it and sat back down in his chair. The fire flared up brightly. He became lost in thought.

Frank hunted for the right words. He wondered about the beliefs he should adopt and how to include them in his re-affirmation. All of it seemed muddled together without edges or clarity. He thought about Meg and about Robert. 'I need to be more open to life. Don't sweat the small stuff. Learn to savor as many moments as I can. Life is to be enjoyed, and the choice whether or not I enjoy my life … is entirely up to me.'

Enjoy your life. Meg said so much with those words. If I'm open to life does that mean I'm open to love? I wonder what she meant. I guess the only way to find out is to go back to Bert's restaurant. I've gotta see Meg again.'

Frank looked up at the night sky. The moon hung in the west. The brightest stars were visible but many more would appear after the moon set. The cool cloudless summer night calmed him. He felt a sense of yearning grow within him for Robert, for his family, and … for Meg. He couldn't wait for tomorrow. He felt so alive.

He looked up to see a bright shooting star as it blazed across the sky.

"Sweet."

Excerpts from
FRANK'S BULLETIN BOARD

Rules for Living Well

One—Take good care of yourself. Do all the things you know you should do, like drink plenty of water, get enough rest, eat good foods; exercise regularly and set time aside for deep thought and/ or meditation. "Common sense is not so common."

Two—Find your purpose; live in harmony with your purpose. Live and work with intention and a sense of purpose. Live your life and do your duty, always keeping the end in mind. Discovering our core purpose helps us achieve life balance.

This is a quote from a book by Kevin McCarthy, *The On-Purpose Person*. "Purpose is the single most motivating force there is. Discover your purpose, be on-purpose, and you will have a life filled with meaning and significance."

Three—Choose the virtues and principles that you believe in and live by them. Plato wrote of four guiding virtues; <u>justice</u> is the virtue of balance and order. <u>Wisdom</u> is the virtue of the mind; it is analytical; it helps one decide how to respond justly to life. <u>Character</u> is who we are. It has to do with honor and integrity. <u>Competence</u> is our abilities. The skills we acquire and the habits we foster add to our competence. Competence has to do with our results when they are in harmony with our principles and values.

Four—Be Impeccable with your Word. (from *The Four Agreements* by Ruiz.) It means living a life of integrity toward others, as well as toward yourself. (Don't believe the lies you tell yourself.)

Five—Always do your best. (again from *The Four Agreements*) Strive to learn, to grow, to contribute. If you always strive to do your best you will never find fault with yourself. If others find fault with you and you know you've done your best then you are free to search for the truth. Find the best way to do something and cultivate good habits.

Six—Don't assume anything. Always keep an open mind. Seek first to understand (from the *Seven Habits of Highly Effective People* by Steven Covey and *The Four Agreements*). Things are never black and white; learn to look for the grey.

Seven—Think; contemplate your world and your place in the world. Analyze and review your beliefs and your habits. Change anything that does not support you. "Lord give me the courage to change the things which can and ought to be changed, the serenity to accept the things which cannot be changed, and the wisdom to know the difference."

Eight—Be grateful for everything. Life is a miracle; you are unique; cultivate a sense of wonder. Laugh everyday.

Nine—Try to live without expectation. There can be no disappointment without expectation. Be open to the possibilities.

Ten—Live a life of service. Be a giver not a taker. Blessed are those who give of themselves for they shall know the kingdom of heaven. As the Beatles said, "The love you get is equal to the love you give."

Excerpts from FRANK'S BULLETIN BOARD

Recommended Books
(In no particular order)

Man's Search for Meaning—Victor Frankl

The Seven Habits of Highly Effective People—Stephen Covey

The Essential Wooden—John Wooden

Emotional Intelligence—Daniel Goleman

Working with Emotional Intelligence—Daniel Goleman

The Book of Five Rings—Miyamoto Musashi

The Way of the Peaceful Warrior—Dan Millman

The Power of Now—Eckhart Tolle

The Art of Happiness—The Dalai Lama

East of Eden—John Steinbeck

The On-Purpose Person—Kevin McCarthy

The Four Agreements—Don Miguel Ruiz

A Guide to Living in the Truth—Michael Casey

A Christmas Carol—Charles Dickens

Attitude is Everything—Keith Harrell

The Doors of Perception—Aldous Huxley

Service at Its Best—Paul Paz

The Lazy Man's Guide to Enlightenment—Thaddeus Golas

Concentration—Ernest Wood

The Power of Empathy—Arthur P. Ciaramicoli and Katherine Ketcham

Unlimited Power—Anthony Robbins

Getting to Yes—Roger Fisher and William Ury

Understanding Oriental Philosophy—James K. Feiblman

Instant Emotional Healing—Peter Lambrou and George Pratt

The Power of Your Subconscious Mind—Dr. Joseph Murphy

The Fifth Discipline—Peter Senge

"Yes or No" —Spencer Johnson

To Do Doing Done—G. Lynne Snead and Joyce Wycoff

The Hobbit—J. R. R. Tolkien

Peak Performers—Charles Garfield

The Odyssey—Homer

The Killer Angels—Michael Shaara

The Hidden Dimension—Edward T. Hall

The Power of Self-Esteem—Nathaniel Brandon

Demian—Herman Hesse

Shiatsu Therapy—Toru Namikoshi

The Official Guide to Success—Tom Hopkins

Paterno by the Book—Joe Paterno

The Left Hand of Darkness—Ursula K. LeGuin

The Seven Principles for Making Marriage Work—John Gottman

Band of Brothers—Stephen E. Ambrose

Signing Their Lives Away—Denise Kiernan and Joseph D'Agnese

A Peoples History of the United States—Howard Zinn

Stranger in a Strange Land—Robert Heinlein

Spontaneous Healing—Andrew Weil

The Seven Spiritual Laws of Yoga—Deepak Chopra

Meditation for Beginners—Jack Kornfield

Prescription for Nutritional Healing—James F. Balch and Phyllis A. Balch

Touch for Health—John Thie and Matthew Thie

Deep Writing—Eric Maisel

Team of Rivals—Doris Kearns Goodwin

How Fiction Works—James Wood

Get Fit Massage—Gill Tree

Huckleberry Finn—Mark Twain

The Red Badge of Courage—Stephen Crane

Cold Mountain-Charles Frazier

Excerpts from FRANK'S BULLETIN BOARD

Recommended Movies
(In no particular order)

The Fifth Element
Saving Private Ryan (we all need to 'earn this')
Gettysburg
The Princess Bride
Young Frankenstein
Don Juan Demarco
Bicentennial Man
Forrest Gump
Open Range
The Kidd
Phenomenon
Groundhog Day
It's a Wonderful Life
Remember the Titans
Rain Man
The Last Samurai
Second Hand Lions
Gandhi
Under the Tuscan Sun
We Were Soldiers
Wizard of Oz
Jack
Patch Adams
Kung Fu Panda
Shrek
Dances with Wolves
Willow

Lord of the Rings Trilogy
The Green Mile

For additional Excerpts from the Bulletin Board and to see pictures of places visited in the book go to grandpasjourneybook. com.

For more from the author visit agdagnese.com.

To find out more about a powerful meditation aid visit eocinstitute.org.

About The Author

A. G. D'Agnese was raised in Rockaway Beach, New York. He marched with the Saint Camillus Band for twelve years. He graduated from Brooklyn Prep in 1972 and from Baruch College CUNY in 1977 where he lettered in fencing for four years. A sales professional for most of his career, he eventually became a sales trainer, drawing inspiration for 'Grandpa's Journey' from many different training seminars. He lives in Roseburg, Oregon. He continues to play the trumpet as a hobby and plays Taps for veterans' funerals. An active member of the Roseburg Lions Club, he also teaches fencing at the YMCA as a volunteer, swims daily, and enjoys football and hunting when in season.

Made in the USA
Coppell, TX
09 December 2021

67697123R00156